New Giants Rising

How Leaders Can Help People and Companies Grow During the Followership Crisis

New Giants Rising

How Leaders Can Help People and Companies Grow During the Followership Crisis

Paul Fisher

Routledge
Taylor & Francis Group
A PRODUCTIVITY PRESS BOOK

Routledge
Taylor & Francis Group
711 Third Avenue, New York, NY 10017

Printed on acid-free paper

International Standard Book Number-13: 978-0-8153-7796-2 (Hardback)
International Standard Book Number-13: 978-1-138-62649-2 (Paperback)
International Standard Book Number-13: 978-1-3152-2817-4 (eBook)

Library of Congress Cataloging in Publication Data

Names: Fisher, Paul D., author.
Title: New giants rising : how leaders can help people and companies grow during the followership crisis / Paul D. Fisher.
Description: New York : Taylor & Francis, [2018] | Includes bibliographical references and index.
Identifiers: LCCN 2017054458| ISBN 9781138626492 (pbk. : alk. paper) | ISBN 9780815377962 (hardback : alk. paper) | ISBN 9781315228174 (eBook)
Subjects: LCSH: Corporations—Growth. | Crisis management. | Leadership.
Classification: LCC HD2746 .F57 2018 | DDC 658.4/06—dc23
LC record available at https://lccn.loc.gov/2017054458
Typeset in ITC Garamond Std
by diacriTech, Chennai

Visit the Taylor & Francis Web site at
http://www.taylorandfrancis.com

and the Productivity Press Web site at
http://www.ProductivityPress.com

Colleen! Look!

You
were
right!

It really IS getting brighter out!!!

Contents

Acknowledgments

It's been a long, strange trip from writing *Beyond the Days of the Giants* in 2013 to *New Giants Rising* here in 2018. At its start, my authoring coach Laurie Harper taught me how not to write like a jerk. In its middle, my speaking coach Kathy Crandall taught me how to stop talking like one. And best of all, just before I started writing *New Giants Rising*, my daughter Anne Fisher explained to me that it might be a good idea if I stopped thinking like one too.

My editor, Erik Hane, made *New Giants Rising* possible through his willingness to dig into that thinking with me—even when, at times, it seemed delusional to both of us.

And at long last I need to publicly thank my colleague, friend, and managing partner, Loren Viere. None of my work would exist had he not created such a challenging environment at our firm. Without it, I never would have found the resolve to define the reason to grow of a new profession—and the emerging decision economy that it is learning to serve.

Colleen, I'll see you at the Tower of London.

About the Author

Paul Fisher spent the first half of his career as a practicing CPA and office leader in a large Twin Cities accounting firm. In 2011, he left the accounting profession to follow a higher purpose: to help people and organizations grow together. He is the author of *Beyond the Days of the Giants* and *New Giants Rising: How Leaders Can Help People and Organizations Grow During the Followership Crisis*.

A thought leader on the concept of followership, Paul believes that the only way for people and organizations to grow in the future is to have a loyal and committed following inside and outside of organizations. Through his research, he discovered that this loyalty and commitment is only possible when all stakeholders embrace a *followership mindset*—a significant paradigm shift in a world focused on *leadership*.

Paul is on a relentless mission to inspire hope, happiness, and growth in the people that live inside our organizations by building a global followership movement. His purpose is to empower them through the followership mindset—one that reconsiders the needs of people to share a purpose, redefines the meaning of value creation as social mobility, and redesigns the growth model with meaningful work.

After a decades-long hiatus from his early days as a rock musician, Paul is getting the band back together to go out on the road—but this time with followership.

Introduction

When I left my accounting practice in 2011, I was asked what I hoped to accomplish by writing books about the continuing success of my colleagues. I said that I intended to define the growth imperative for my profession for the next 75 years. A growth imperative, any given profession's reason to grow, is ultimately where succession lives—society needing us more every year than it did the last. As people, the relevance and meaning of our lives hinge on our persistence in providing social mobility to ourselves and one another. We do this by buying, selling, and consuming one another's goods and services in meaningful ways that create a pattern of rising growth. And we are no different from any other part of the economy today in search of the holy grail of personal and organizational growth.

Despite our timeless human need to express commitment, loyalty, and accountability to one another inside these successful social mobility systems, to grow together, young colleagues are increasingly disconnecting from our firms. And for the few that do pursue the path to partnership, the call is to accountability to our current social mobility foundations. The narrative is, "We've got a system of growth. It isn't working well. But it's all we've got, so we're asking you to try harder and be accountable to make it work." Succession has become a slow and painful death march for some of us—leading directly to the merger and consolidation movement.

But the more interesting thoughts on the issue came from those not interested in pursuing partnership, those who don't care at all about the financial capital maintenance system of succession. These people felt highly accountable to a successful system of social mobility, but one that extended well beyond their firms' borders. Words like equality, sustainability, relevance, and meaning were at the top of their minds as the means to achieve the very same goal of growth and social mobility for all.

The concept of social capital kept popping up as the mechanism that bound all this together. As I looked at it more deeply, our succession crisis began to look less and less like an intergenerational conflict, as it is so often painted. Instead, it began to look more and more like two separate and distinct systems of social mobility, supported by two completely different social capital foundations. This observation became the heartbeat of *New Giants Rising*: something much bigger is going on than simply a generation of young people refusing to define themselves like their parents.

The search was on then for the "reason to grow" that our new generations will use to create the future of social mobility and meaningful work in their profession. This included examining the traditional role of accounting, and how it supported decision-making for financial capital during the twentieth century. That examination revealed the much bigger picture of how rising social capital foundations broaden people's social mobility inside each historical cycle of industrial regeneration by allowing people to successfully adapt to newer, more isolating workplace environments—and grow together as a result. The adaptations of people to that socio-industrial regeneration cycle, which I've termed the Followership Cycle, became the key to decoding the future relevance of what is now becoming the decision-support profession.

The process of discovery about our reason to grow, and writing about it, gave me an even bigger revelation, though: not only had I defined the reason to grow for a profession, but by extension, the reason to grow for the global economy in the twenty-first century. It became very clear to me that the social-capital foundations of the twentieth-century Consumption Economy were giving way to the social-capital foundations of the twenty-first-century decision economy.

It's painfully obvious that growth from the Consumption Economy has stalled as a direct result of the death of twentieth-century social capital. The rising middle class that this economy produced began to erode at the beginning of the most recent industrial regeneration in the mid-1970s, and that erosion has gotten worse ever since as productivity and wages continued to stagnate. We can see that decay everywhere: in the recently severe friction between our political parties, among nations, and inside institutions we specifically built to define, grow, and defend our shared social priorities. The social glue of the twentieth century is failing in very important and seemingly permanent ways.

But it's not all bleak. Against this backdrop, the social-capital foundations of the new decision economy are quietly forming. They are the future of social mobility and a new rising middle class that will bring unprecedented growth and prosperity in the coming century. The feelings of isolation and irrelevance we feel today are merely the calm before the storm of spectacular growth and relevance for our New Giants. With the onset of artificial intelligence, that time will come very quickly now. And with that new technology, we can speed up the arrival of twenty-first-century social capital—for the benefit of all.

Chapter 1

New Giants Rising

The generational divide that has long existed in our economy is now growing alarmingly wider. We all feel it: young people trying to gain a foothold in their professional lives while previous generations quietly believe its new, younger colleagues are too self-involved and uncommitted to cultivate the relationships that they're leaving behind at retirement. It's a problem that sits at the intersection of historic and economic forces that stretch far beyond problems of workplace culture in professional service firms. And it's also a problem that stretches to my dinner table.

My daughter Anne and I share a profession. She's a young senior manager at a large accounting firm, a field I worked in for decades; because of this, work is always on the tip of our tongues. However, something interesting happens whenever the conversation turns toward our professional lives: our father–daughter familiarity disappears, and I suddenly become less her father and more just one more of the older white-male, upper-management types around which she might typically guard herself. Whatever social capital we've built between us as family members falls away.

But Anne *has* shared with me pieces of her workplace experience. I know she's acutely aware of the political surroundings at her office, but would rather just work and let others do the gossiping about who's carrying whose water. Or who calls the shots at the office. Or whether people are being promoted or treated fairly. Or if clients are happy, or if colleagues are supporting one another. She *sees and feels* all these things and surely has deeply held opinions, but she doesn't share them, especially not with me. She is busy, and such discussions don't contribute to the operational life she prefers, one in which she has control and is able to focus on the multitude of tasks at hand, free of idle speculation. She's got a role, and she's going to perform it; it's as simple as that.

This compartmentalized approach to her work life probably sounds familiar to any young person in any line of work. But it stands in stark contrast to how most of us conduct our lives away from our jobs. In our personal lives, we easily share roles that are typical in an evolving family dynamic. For instance, I have the difficult and unenviable job of trying to find ways to make my grandson Simon like me as much as he likes Anne, his mother. Her job is much different: while I'm trying to curry favor with him by saying "yes" to him all the time, she has to say "no" to him pretty frequently. Despite this, he still seems to like her a lot more than he likes me. That's because they are at the core of the family's operational future and, as such, are the most relevant to one another. No amount of happy cheerleading by Simon's Grampa will elevate him to the degree of relevance that they share as mother and son.

But despite all the potential for family conflict, we manage to stay on the same page because we share *purpose*, personified by our young Simon. Everything flows from that. All our efforts are focused in the same direction—the continued genetic, financial, and social success of our family. Our *persistence* in cooperating with one another in operational matters and family succession is fueled by that important goal despite our differing jobs—our specialties, if you will—and despite our age difference. This feels so natural and ingrained that we never give it any real thought at all. And yet, the moment *work* comes up between my daughter and me, all this shared purpose falls away. That same dynamic is almost wholly absent from our professional lives.

In our business lives, with me as a former equity partner and her as a current senior manager, we are unable to seamlessly talk about work in our shared profession. This is because we have no shared higher purpose—like Simon is to our family—to bind us in common cause. This disconnect at first appears generational, a divide between the old guard and young people. But if that were truly the case, we would feel that same discomfort in our personal lives where we interact with members of different generations all the time. But we don't. We easily share personal family purpose while failing to share professional purpose.

I remember once telling Anne about a group of managing partners that I'd organized in Minneapolis. We spent meetings discussing leadership challenges, and I was enthused about the conclusion we came to: that we would all need each other someday. Anne, however, was unimpressed.

"That's nice, Dad," was about all the response I got. She would later refer to this group as my "managing partners club." Even between a loving dad and daughter, the suspicion that fuels the *appearance* of a generational divide was clear: to her, my meetings with others in my position were a sign of exclusion, a banding together of the old guard. The shared higher purpose so easily felt in our family was simply absent from her thinking about us as professional colleagues.

The reason behind this strange inconsistency between our personal and business lives lies in something called social capital. It accumulates over time and, if successfully invested, can produce more and more benefit as it grows. A social capital system is successful when people demonstrate *persistence* in their pursuit of common goals. Those mutually beneficial goals are what keep people engaged and what hold the system in place. But when stress reduces people's willingness and ability to pursue those common goals, social capital stops growing and begins to deplete. If this goes on for long enough, the system itself enters a state of peril, as we see today in our slowly growing economy and profession.

The most useful definition of social capital in the twentieth century was created by French philosopher Pierre Bourdieu. Specifically, he referred to social capital as being comprised of "durable networks of people," the growth of which created rising economic activity. Interpersonal relationships in the workplace lasted a long time, as did the trusted brands that our economy produced. Today however, the appearance of a generational divide suggests that these networks of people aren't durable at all. People simply aren't showing relationship persistence the same way they did in the past to pursue common goals and their benefits. The symptoms are obvious: leaders across many industries are experiencing what they perceive as declining loyalty of customers, and the declining commitment of employees.

Why, though? Why are the same durable networks of people that served individuals and the economy well throughout the past century proving inadequate to meet the needs of our new generations? The answer to that comes from looking at the history of how the formation of social capital changes during each new major industrial regeneration. We'll call it the Followership Cycle; it forces us to adapt to one another's needs inside newer and more isolating technology environments.

Common sense tells us that, in our new world of specialization and global labor and material sourcing, the durability of specific groups of people couldn't have led growth any longer. We may be more connected to the world than ever before, but we're also more isolated as individuals; far less frequently are our colleagues just one workstation over on the assembly line. A more modern and realistic understanding of social-capital formation today must remove the notion of these outdated networks. There must be a more useful and richly rewarding way to pursue purpose together in a world where many of us can't even see one another any longer.

So, while durable networks of people helped generations of the prior century achieve a rising middle class, they are woefully inadequate to the task of creating persistence of purpose in a new century. Common cause must be formed around something other than permanent interpersonal relationships. And it will fall to new leaders to foster that binding common cause—except the nature of who's doing the leading is changing too.

Certainly, the leaders of our future exist in the ranks of young professionals and even current students. But by that, I don't mean the future leaders of our profession are buried somewhere in that population of young people and that a select few of them will emerge someday to lead their colleagues. Instead, they will *all* lead. *Every single one of them. All the time.*

But how can that be? People my age, who grew up in the 1960s and spent a career enjoying the fruits of a successful leadership past, are almost certainly saying: if *everyone* is a leader, doesn't that mean no one is? It doesn't sound like a leadership strategy at all; it sounds leaderless. While that person is, in one sense, correct, it's this intergenerational handwringing that lies at the heart of the divide between young and old members of society, between a depleting social capital system and the emerging new one starting to grow. And this handwringing has led to stereotypes of young people, rather than understanding, adaptation, and human progress.

Popular business culture frequently invents stereotypes to tidy up the messy business of being human. So, rather than dig in to the underlying sociology to find the real reasons that a reimagined foundation for the tools of leadership is quite necessary and a natural progression of our current century's Followership Cycle, business culture has invented the "Millennial." We all know the profile; it exists to help explain why young people appear to be failing to produce what we traditionally think of as leaders capable of rallying the growth of durable networks of people. Using "Millennial" lets people classify a whole generation by their perceived behavior to explain negative changes in workplace productivity. Unfortunately, using profiling to understand, modify, or adapt behavior is sort of like trying to explain and cope with the common cold by analyzing sneezing and sniffling. It is useless as a tool to help people adapt to their surroundings and to one another.

But this creation of categories *does* tell us what the people who created them think, and so it's an important starting point as we explore what a "leaderless" culture might mean. The Millennial profile is described as entitled and narcissistic, their attitudes in the workplace thought of as disrespectful of authority and dismissive of the chain of command. They want their input and ideas to be heard immediately, instead of wading through political channels for years before making significant contributions. They are not, this thinking goes, interested in waiting their turn.

And with all these apparently widespread personality defects come the need to find someone to blame. So, the deficiencies of a new generation are attributed to soft and overinvolved parenting. Popular urban mythology relays horrifying stories of moms attending job interviews with their basement-dwelling adult children. These stories are obviously exaggerated; but worse, they're completely unhelpful in telling us how people can be led to persistently follow one another in pursuit of common goals today. That's the only adaptive reason human behavior changes at all in an economy. People want to follow other people but they're struggling to do that today.

This impulse to classify generations is a problem worth addressing. It's an instinct that leads older generations to explain any behavior that doesn't support durable networks of people, the outdated foundation of social-capital formation, as something that needs to be fixed. And it suggests to us too that traditional concepts of trust, teamwork, and relationship building, as we knew them in the twentieth century, are automatically good because they promote the creation and maintenance of those durable networks.

But the reality is that durable networks of people are in the final death throes of their usefulness in the creation and accumulation of social capital; as such, judging Millennials by their unwillingness to cultivate them is less than useful. It also ignores the reality that such words as "trust," "teamwork," and "relationship" will need to be completely redefined in any new social-capital environment that can be expected to produce persistence of effort in ways other than relationship permanence. As we will soon see, the only thing this stereotyping really shows us is how and why durable networks of people were so effective at producing rising labor productivity along with a rising middle class in the first seventy-five years of the twentieth century, and by extension, why they'll be so ineffective at producing similar personal and organizational growth now.

In truth, current and future generations' ability to grow personally, professionally, and organizationally *together* has nothing to do with generational behavioral deficits. It has solely to do with a lack of persistence in pursuing the *same* goals. Both sides of what we think of as the generational divide are trying to grow social capital by pursuing purpose. On one hand, older generations are trying to sustain durable networks of people as the binding force for persistence of joint effort. On the other hand, newer generations are leaving those networks in search of higher forms of social capital that will help them meet their needs as human beings in a far more dehumanizing work environment. The social-capital environment a young person navigates looks far different than the one a baby boomer entered; it's a dehumanizing technological landscape the likes of which the prior generation could never have imagined. Refusing to mold themselves according to the workplace social capital standards of their parents isn't failure to thrive—it's future survival.

Rather than being behavioral flaws, the current generation's adaptations to the stresses of today's productivity environment are completely in line with Maslow's higher order human need for recognizing and valuing one's unique self. What is typically characterized as Millennial narcissism is a reach for that next-higher order of needs: self-esteem, achievement, recognition, independence, and prestige. As we'll see, looking to rise a level in Maslow's hierarchy is a historically normal adaptive response to each new industrial regeneration. In truth, these new Followership phenomena are more appropriately described as *socio*-industrial regeneration cycles.

So, what appears to be a lack of persistence in pursuing group goals is, in truth, *extraordinary* persistence in pursuing the formation of modern social capital required for the foundation of Followership Agreements capable of producing global growth. When examined this way, we see that Millennials are actively pursuing the same goal every generation has chased since the beginning of recorded time—a better, more rewarding future for themselves and their children.

This technology-induced need for the formation of more effective social capital is reshaping the concept of leadership. But consider this persistent new idea of *everyone* being a leader. What does that mean, and why is it happening?

Almost no project today involves the exact same network of people inside an organization. This is because almost no modern individual or organizational problem can be solved without a newly formed specialist team ready to face a unique set of complex conditions. Durable networks of people don't work anymore, simply because a single network of people is not able to complete the wide variety of specialized tasks facing modern organizations looking to meet increasingly complex needs. This is a normal output of highly specialized people collaborating in a global environment.

Within a workplace, this trend toward specialization has multiple consequences. First, it's far more frequent now for employees of the same company, perhaps even members of the same team, to have entirely separate sets of expertise. Specialists are brought in to deal with a specific task, rarely collaborating on a problem as much as eventually handing it off once their specific action item has been addressed. This drastically cuts down on the need for coworkers to be familiar with one another, in either a personal or professional sense; it's easy to see how feelings of isolation could set in.

But it also means that it becomes far tougher for a single person to be "in charge" of all these disparate specialists. It's nearly impossible for any one person to hand down purpose and meaning from on high. So, specialists are forced to "lead" themselves, to create their own purpose and meaning in an emerging, and confusing to some of us, "leaderless" reality that will redefine how shared purpose is cultivated, how quality is negotiated, and how accountability is expressed among people in global companies.

That truth is uncomfortable for everyone involved in leadership. But rather than look to the source of the problem, negative social-capital growth, we continue to promote the tools we used to grow durable networks of people and hope that some future generation will produce leaders again as we knew them during the twentieth century. This inability to help serve the very real leadership needs of people in our increasingly dehumanizing world of technology is one of the defining challenges of the twenty-first century. And it won't be solved by continuing to patch together our declining twentieth-century social capital.

It's clear that we sit at a moment of profound socioeconomic change. As we see in our own political processes here in the United States, there is now severe pressure to make progress on job creation and economic growth. This pressure has reached politically explosive proportions globally as well, as the most developed of our nation-states find themselves facing revolt by large swaths of their populations who don't feel included in the small pockets of prosperity that do exist. There is certainly a thriving middle class, but it is not a *rising* middle class.

There is a human side to this socioeconomic fracturing that goes far beyond our citizens' relative success at acquiring wealth and income. When people produced and consumed goods and services in the middle of the twentieth century, they felt *good* about themselves, their employers, and their trusted brands. All our institutions, including businesses, experienced the benefit of those durable networks of people in much the same way that they experienced their family lives.

This comfort and security does not exist today. While it's normal to want to return to these past emotional foundations of personal and organizational growth, the history of socio-industrial regeneration, which we'll call a "Followership Cycle," shows us that we cannot go backward. We must follow our new generations to the future for which they have so persistently prepared themselves. The history of the Followership Cycle paints a very different picture of how new generations will lead our now-global economy. That socio-industrial regeneration phenomenon, and the "Followership Agreements," or social contracts, that propel them, is the true driver of social behavioral change. Understanding Followership's history, and our current place in that repeated cycle, is critical to understanding how we will serve one another's needs in the future.

That Followership Cycle consists of three phases, the first of which is when **technology follows technology.** This phase of industrial regeneration begins when economic growth is led by the creation and expansion of the new elements of a new industrial infrastructure. This growth phase during the last two cycles lasted roughly twenty-five years each. For example, during the stretch between 1850 and 1875, Rockefeller's oil and Carnegie's steel led the race to build new infrastructure around the country, creating expensive new technologies and driving economic growth. In more modern times between 1975 and 2000, it was Gates's software and Jobs's hardware that served the same purpose.

Both these periods were followed by a twenty-five-year stretch in which economic growth was fueled by **people following technology.** In short, people moved to fill the new jobs created by these new industries and technologies. Between 1875 and 1900, mass migration of people to cities, where the jobs were newly available, created successes such as Henry Ford's auto factories in Detroit. But as people "moved to Detroit," the dawning of the Gilded Age revealed a darker side to technological innovation. People were reluctant to let go of many of the practices based on social capital of the previous Followership Cycle. For example, children worked alongside their parents in factories, a practice that came from their previous agrarian lives where working in the fields with one's parents was a normal part of a successful socioeconomic unit.

This second phase of the Followership Cycle, when people begin trying to adapt to the new social landscape created by their new technologies, is full of mismatched social capital practices such as this. This is when some people hold tightly to past forms of social capital formation even as they become outdated and detrimental to their own success. That should sound relevant because it is: this is the phase we currently find ourselves in where social upheaval is revealing our own Second Gilded Age.

In our own time, starting around 2000, **people followed technology** through global labor and material sourcing. No longer limited by time and space, technology was suddenly able to pursue all the inputs of business—people, materials, and information—without regard to geography. But just as in the Followership Cycle before it, this Second Gilded Age reveals our own inability to let go of the social capital of our past. This is what fuels economic nationalism today and its negative global economic growth implications. And while it's a normal human response of people wishing they could restore their past, it hampers the inclusivity needed to foster the growth that will be necessary for any nation to succeed in a global economy. This phenomenon slows the process of building the newer, more effective Followership Agreements that these new technologies require—the agreements that will help us make progress toward an economy that works for everyone.

This second phase of Followership is always tumultuous because, as alluring as it is, technology alone dehumanizes us. Any new technology is first implemented without regard for how it will affect the people who will occupy the jobs it creates. This is a normal part of industrial regeneration. The predominant form of capital that serves wealth creation is preoccupied with itself, first and foremost. It is only after the effects of dehumanization appear that capital must deal with them as a matter of its own survival. And that time has arrived. The reality today is that a leadership call for people to follow technology is no more profoundly innovative than the call 125 years earlier for people to "move to Detroit." Without accompanying social capital that rises to the challenge of a more isolated and disconnected labor force, people feel like industrial commodities—irrelevant and interchangeable.

Today's generations have made enormous progress adapting to the productivity requirements of their futures. They've adopted—or "followed"—new technologies almost seamlessly, a critical step that has raised unit productivity exponentially. But unit productivity, defined as our ability to produce lots more of what we produced before, tends to simply drive prices down, as opposed to raising the value of our work. Raising the value of our work requires getting people to "follow" not just technology, but other people. This must happen in a consistent and accelerating manner, and people must *persist* in doing so, despite the death today of the durable networks of people that served workplace persistence in the past.

True rising labor productivity—and a rising middle class—happens during the third and final phase of the Followership Cycle, when **people follow people**. After any new technology infrastructure is built, new process technologies must also be deployed to make the best use of it. However, alongside those processes meant to make our technology more efficient, the needs of people dictate that we also generate higher forms of social capital to buffer the isolating effects of the new process technologies. Human beings must believe that there is a joint cooperative purpose to their efforts, despite seeing no direct evidence of it around them. This fuels their willingness to persist in what are fundamentally dehumanizing environments, and it is what our current leadership practices have yet to deal with effectively.

As an example, take modern assembly line processes in the early twentieth century. As individuals in the workforce began to suffer the stresses of isolation in their regimented, linear production lines, concepts such as love and belonging began to permeate churches, homes, workplaces, and marriages. Emotional security became a socioeconomic requirement, as our institutions began to make it a priority in the means they used to govern, manage labor, create brands, and define social priorities.

Today, while cloud technologies increase the speed at which people can perform tasks, there are corresponding productivity dangers. We are less connected by function, time, or space than at any point in history. And outdated Followership Agreements based on Maslow's middle order of needs for love, relatedness, and belonging are now completely inadequate to address a world where people can't see and often don't even know one another. And now, facing the onset of artificial intelligence, our Followership Agreements must quickly move toward serving the more elevated human needs of self-actualization and personal fulfillment to effectively adapt to the stresses of technology.

Luckily, we are very close to a new period of rising labor productivity that will dwarf its twentieth-century counterpart, as the foundation of social capital moves further up Maslow's hierarchy in response to that increased worker isolation. But because relatively few leaders will build the Followership Agreements of the twenty-first century, the social capital that those leaders create will devour the financial capital of the businesses of those that choose to ignore it. The history of Followership proves that **the needs of people** will prevail. Whether it was Ford's assembly lines, today's cloud technologies, or tomorrow's artificial intelligence, labor process innovations demand *rising* forms of social capital, if labor productivity is going to lead economic growth. **People must follow people** again. Once they do, the payoff is big, and it promises to change our new century in a profound way.

During the twentieth century, businesses hired people and proceeded to engage in transactions to create the social capital of durable networks of people through Followership Agreements based on Maslow's middle order of needs. Because of this, businesses effectively owned social capital in the form of workforce-in-place and customer lists that were considered solid business assets then. In effect, financial capital was the *creator and acquirer* of social capital.

Those days are gone forever.

Quite the reverse of that, in our new century, *social capital is the creator and acquirer of financial capital.* Rather than organizations serving as the structures through which people find security and belonging, they will instead be forced to adapt those structures to serve the personal growth needs of the members of their Followership Agreements. This provides a very real way to think about our current social-capital standoff on the brink of Followership change. One side of the divide is holding all the financial capital produced in the twentieth century, and the other side is holding the growing body of twenty-first-century social capital. Successful organizations are starting to figure out how to navigate this divide, and highly visible examples are easy to find.

Few companies have paid as close attention to the Followership Cycle and responded as quickly to it as Apple. They've been among the first to recognize each new phase, identifying when different sources of growth are almost tapped out and quickly moving on to lead new growth. And by defining Followership as it unfolds, they are creating social capital.

During the first part of the Followership Cycle, where **technology followed technology**, Apple designed and produced arguably the best personal computer in the marketplace. It was a product for its time. The personal computer was a foundational piece of the new digital infrastructure being built, and it predictably led growth.

During today's phase, as **people follow technology**, their seminal product offering is one that has helped shape the world to such an extent that few of us can imagine a time without it: the modern cell phone. The iPhone has begun to prepare the world for the coming day when **people follow people** again, as people gain the ability to negotiate common sets of beliefs and connections on a personal level in real time, from anywhere. People have access to all the ideas the world has to offer, whether personal, political, creative, or otherwise, and the ability to contact whoever we want about them, regardless of our spot on the map. Crucially, this capacity will soon help people crowdsource shared purpose in their work lives as well, replacing durable networks of people as the foundation of social capital. This will mark the real start of the construction of twenty-first-century social capital.

Most of the way through that second phase in the cycle, the person responsible for *defining purpose* at Apple Computer, and driving the design and production of its flagship products, was its founder, Steve Jobs. He is a towering example of leadership in recent history and we still look to him today to define CEO greatness.

On the other hand, Tim Cook, who succeeded Jobs as CEO, is faced with a different challenge. His leadership is quite different in form and substance from Jobs because Apple has recognized that CEOs can't hand down purpose from on high. Instead, he must be a leader in a leaderless environment, defending the purpose others have created for themselves. To be successful in this new phase, future redesigns of Apple's flagship products, as well as the genesis of its new ones, will require more than just functionality and style. They will need to serve a *purpose* that inspires people to *persistently* produce, buy, and use their products to the exclusion of their competitors' products, most of which are now technologically equal.

But this crowdsourced sharing of purpose is messy and sometimes downright ugly, as we have seen in the recent round of electoral politics in the United States. This is because not everyone agrees with any given statement of purpose. For example, when Tim Cook was ordered by the U.S. District Courts to release code to investigators of the San Bernardino terrorism attack, he refused. He had to defend personal privacy despite polling at the time that suggested only about 50 percent of people in the United States felt it was the right decision.

His decision could have nothing to do with his personal beliefs and everything to do with the beliefs of Apple's Followership stakeholders. His job wasn't to create that purpose as a "leader" might have done; it was to defend the "leaderless" purpose already being created by current and future owners of its products. So, framed through the lens of "leaderless" social capital, successful CEOs of the next seventy-five years will not be the great *definers*-of-purpose as we saw in the twentieth century, the CEO that Steve Jobs was, but they will be the great *defenders* of purpose, as crowdsourced in the Followership marketplace. The successful companies of the twenty-first century will be, in the traditional sense of the concept, leaderless. And it will be no different for people—leaders—in the global economy.

In the current Followership Cycle, people are very nearly done following technology. The new global and digital infrastructure has been created, and people have moved to fill the jobs created by that technology. People are ready to start following people again, just as the historical pattern tells us they should. Those of us in current generations who "moved to Detroit," those who successfully followed technology and benefitted from the higher wages and better living standards provided for them there, are being prepared for a true purpose that is far beyond making our own lives more meaningful and rewarding. They are preparing themselves to make a significant contribution to the lives of others who are suffering in Middle America and other parts of the developing world—the people who didn't "move to Detroit."

Maslow's theory of human need tells us that just beyond those pesky needs for individualism, self-regard, and importance so persistently pursued by our newer generations lies the real prize, the pinnacle of human growth: self-actualization. The hallmark developmental traits of *true morality, lack of prejudice, and acceptance of fact* are those that will propel our New Giants, the future leaders of industries, to that place. And through their work toward creating leaderless Followership Agreements, Millennials have been developing exactly those traits in themselves. It positions them perfectly to define our global growth-filled future.

The political landscape of today has brought the Followership Cycle's next phase into crystal-clear focus. Many of the offspring of the people who literally moved to Detroit at the end of the nineteenth century still reside in those cities, and times are hard for some of them: those same industrial hubs that drew them suffered heavy manufacturing losses from those cities, as lower-cost areas of the country began to compete with them. The social cost of that shift severely challenged Detroit, and many of our cities, to adapt to a new reality.

In Middle America today, competition from even lower-cost areas is eroding that transplanted manufacturing base, but this time on an international scale. That social cost presents as the unrest in America today, fueled by the unique experiences of people who are responding normally to their environments based on outdated versions of social capital. Those adhering to the Followership Agreements that produced the social capital of the twentieth century are starting a conversation with those seeking the social capital of the twenty-first century. It's a high-stakes conversation that not everyone is able to hear clearly and respond to effectively.

Despite appearances, this conversation is not a battle between truth and falsehood, intelligence and ignorance, or good and bad. It is the dawn of a new phase of the current Followership Cycle. And it presents our new generations with the opportunity to forge shared higher ideals among people of wildly differing social capital foundations and beliefs. Those beliefs don't come from any definition of inherent morality or righteousness, but from the daily transactions of their economic lives and the institutions that form around them.

But this is difficult to explain to someone who lost his manufacturing job and feels the loss very personally. All he knows, or should know, is that the social support of his place of work and everything that it represented is gone. And because he didn't "move to Detroit" by following technology into a global arena, he is ill-prepared to listen to a new generation of people who seem preoccupied with their own self-worth, importance, and uniqueness as they live comfortable, if unfulfilled, lives inside their specialist cells.

But he *might* be interested in listening to someone who had his best interests at heart and demonstrated not only real concern but real commitment to helping him join a newer, more productive and rewarding place than the one that has left him behind. Someone with real solutions and plans that include him. As people begin to follow people again in this new and important phase of the current Followership Cycle, it is people like these who will help him bridge the gap between the social capital of his past and the social capital of his future. And so that is relevance and meaning for us in the future: to elevate those who've been left behind.

Today, that disconnected factory laborer is tempted to listen first to others who have expressed concern for his plight, but who then promise to bring back the social capital of the twentieth century. This fact lies at the heart of the effectiveness of the slogan of our country's most recent winning presidential campaign, "Make America Great Again," a promise to restore a past life these people feel has gone painfully missing. But while it is *easy* to appeal to the experiences of one side of the social-capital conversation and tell them that they are right, it is *hard* to try to lead people of uniquely different beliefs and experiences to a set of shared ideals, away from the prior social structure of their lives. But that is the challenge of our New Giants. The history of the Followership Cycle proves that any goal less than this will fail to help us move forward as an economy and a nation.

President Obama recently referred to this twenty-first-century social capital as the leverage that all members of our society will need to provide increasingly better lives for themselves and their families: "We're going to have to redesign the social compact in some fairly fundamental ways over the next twenty years." But he cautioned that government can only help create "more of a runway" for economic growth. It cannot create the flight path itself toward a plural and "cohesive society in which productivity and wealth generation are not automatically linked to how many hours you put in." That is the job of our New Giants, and it is the focus of this book.

New Giants Rising will take us through the two most recent historical Followership Cycles, draw parallels between them, and ultimately lay the blueprint for the construction of the social capital of the twenty-first century. The goal is to inform and inspire those new leaders toward the important transformation that is beginning right now, this moment in time when their important contribution to the greater good of a global society is at hand.

Chapter 2

Leaderless

To understand the shift in the sociology of economic growth that's happening, we should start with that concept that confuses so many of us, the one that young people are currently adapting to: what exactly does it mean to be "leaderless," and why should we want it?

We can start to see the answer to this question in some very familiar places. For example, the NFL produced a tagline several years ago that read, "Together, We Make Football." It's a simple twenty-first-century statement of purpose that grants everyone—including its fans—a role and stake in the creation of their product. You would have never seen a slogan like this in the twentieth century; a statement of purpose forty years ago might have been "Our Teams Make Football, Just For You." Fans wouldn't have been involved in shaping the product or its purpose; that would have been handed to them by leaders. But now, rather than leave the consumer out of responsibility for creating their product, the NFL chose to include them as joint stakeholders. Fans now have a role, and as such, they are "leaders" as it relates to the creation and evolution of the NFL's Followership Agreement. It is very much like Apple's effort to defend personal privacy; the company is generating social capital by crowdsourcing inclusion in the direction and identity of the company.

"Together, We Make Football" established the foundation for a crowdsourced, leaderless growth environment. By inviting consumers to participate in the creation of their product, the NFL effectively removed the league from sole responsibility for defining purpose, negotiating quality, and defining accountability, assigning it instead to everyone who produces, consumes, or otherwise partners as a stakeholder with them.

As such, their product would no longer be defined by its tribal leaders, the durable networks of people known as teams, which were led by owners. Instead, it would be governed by new sets of social rules negotiated by its growing audience, which was now effectively crowdsourcing the formation of purpose and the negotiation of quality.

NFL teams long ago had to give up the notion of its own durable networks of people serving as a foundation for its growth. The average tenure of players has rapidly declined over time, such that the quaint notion of player loyalty and fan commitment to teams as an adequate foundation for league growth is now clearly absurd. To grow larger, and to secure better lives for all its stakeholders, the NFL needed a new "reason to grow" as the foundation of its Followership Agreement, a powerful reason that would inspire increasing numbers of people to buy its product, despite the reduction in permanence of its durable networks of people—its teams.

Finding and nurturing this leaderless reason to grow is a challenge facing every industry, organization, and individual business in the world today. It is central to the construction of our new Followership Agreements. Without them, whether it's an entertainment product such as the NFL or far more essential human pursuits, growth will be impossible. One especially important profession has already begun this transition, with striking growth results.

I was listening to a story on National Public Radio (NPR) told by a doctor in which he described a leaderless medical practice scenario. He was describing past emergency room procedures for admission and treatment of near-drowning victims in a cold-water environment. The medical quality team had noted that their number of surviving patients didn't meet national averages for similar admissions nationwide. So, they set out to dissect the process to see if they could do better.

As they analyzed the process, it became apparent that similar sets of circumstances were being addressed inconsistently or differently each time they occurred. The doctor in charge was making process changes on a case-by-case basis, based on what he thought was best for each individual patient. Because of this, he was exercising his judgment differently under nearly identical clinical circumstances. And that made it difficult for the entire team to get a handle on which procedures were working best, and why. In response to that, they began to construct a best-practices approach that could be used across all cases, one that relied far less on judgment calls.

After they started to use the new clinical process, the doctor was no longer required to redesign protocol on a continuous basis and tell each team member what to do. Now that he was no longer required to "direct traffic" like before in the emergency room, he could concentrate on his own performance as a specialist. Far from what we might imagine, as soon as he stopped being "in charge" in a traditional sense, the newly leaderless team saw survival rates skyrocket.

Without a traditional "leader," each team member had an equal stake and authority to participate a process that allowed them to focus purely on their own specialties. No one was in charge anymore; they were "leaderless," because everyone had become a leader.

But, as beneficial as this leaderless process was to patient health, there was a significant emotional loss for everyone involved. In his previous clinical experience, people counted on the doctor to stay engaged in a continuous process of listening to the patient, monitoring his symptoms, and then responding in some way. The doctor would develop a personal connection with the patients, and the patients trusted the doctor more because of it. For example, even the line, "Take two aspirin and call me in the morning," which is just a nice way of saying, "I don't know what's wrong with you," gave comfort to patients, because they felt they were receiving attention from a great leader of medicine with whom they had a relationship.

These days of medicine before it became leaderless had a name. They were called the Days of the Giants, and a doctor's Gianthood was a powerful and rewarding position. Those physicians exercised that great power by dealing in real time with the three essential elements of any Followership Agreement. They could redirect **purpose** of any treatment plan, negotiate **quality** with the patient by listening and responding, and handle the **accountability** of everyone else working in the clinic or hospital at a moment's notice by giving orders to nurses and staff. Patients felt good about medicine and were loyal to their doctors. Nurses were committed to their clinics and hospitals. Everyone felt more secure and connected to one another, wrapped in the social capital cocoon of this intimate and responsive durable network of people.

But the most interesting part of the story about this new clinical process was a seemingly innocuous detail that spoke to the true empowerment of leaderless purpose. When the hospital was alerted that a patient was set to arrive, someone would need to give the order to start the assembly of people and technology in the emergency room, to prepare. But the person giving this order was not the doctor, the *most* empowered person in the room; instead, the decision and orders to set the process in motion were given to a lowly telephone operator, the *least* powerful person in the process.

The entire process was leaderless because the doctor no longer needed to conduct the people-orchestra. Quite the opposite of being the product of only one person's leadership and experience, the leaderless team tapped the combined experience of all their colleagues and patients around the world—effectively crowdsourcing the entire operation. And all that experience and input was distilled down to a protocol that was initiated not by a Giant, but by a telephone operator.

In the absence of purpose handed down by a central authority, specialists in a leaderless team are freed up to focus on what they do best without waiting for judgment calls that aren't always reliable. In an age of rapidly increasing specialization and coworker isolation, it's easy to see why leaderless Followership holds advantages, not only for medicine but any global organization. But as we've seen, that shift doesn't happen overnight; there are leadership frustrations that must be navigated first.

I remember once chatting with a managing partner of a large office in a major city one day. He had a team of around twenty-five young employees working on an installation of an Enterprise Resource Planning system at a client office. I recall making some sort of glowing comment about the wonderful benefits of the new system and the talents of the young people putting it together. At one point, he stopped me and said, "These kids don't *know* anything."

Interestingly, his statement wasn't meant to be dismissive of his young team members' talents, skills, or motivations. He was simply expressing a common frustration held by yesterday's Giants: that there seemed to be no one in charge that had any general business experience to provide oversight, just like our old-fashioned family doctor example above. There was no one to call the shots if the client wasn't happy, and no one on the team seemed to know what the overall goals of the installation were. The beehive was busy and the job was getting done, but there was no one to continually redefine purpose, negotiate quality, or enforce accountability along the way. He felt that someone who knew "what was going on" ought to be "in charge."

His feelings about the process were not without foundation. The seamless sharing of Why, What, and How among people has always been how stuff gets done. The social contracts underlying Followership Agreements have always been the foundation of growth and productivity. But the clarity of the basic motivational needs of people are being blurred by the combined effects of the *death* of twentieth-century Followership Agreements, based on leader-defined purpose, and the simultaneous *rise* of leaderless twenty-first-century Followership Agreements, agreements based on people cooperating with one another to serve a greater purpose together, like in medicine. That dissonance is producing confusion, fear, and frustration that limit our ability to grow as individuals and organizations—or for that matter, as nations.

Leaderless growth works well in medicine today because there is a strong reason to grow that serves as its Followership foundation. It motivates everyone to *persist* in coordinated effort together, despite difficulties experienced along the way and despite the loss of the Giants and their durable networks of people.

Medicine's reason to grow has evolved substantially since it began building the Followership Agreement that includes all its stakeholders: doctors, allied health professionals, patients, and payors. The social goal of medicine, once considered to be the prevention and cure of illness, has come to be described more broadly as the maintenance of health. That *shared* purpose supersedes the *individual* purpose of each member of the Followership Agreement, including any remaining Giants.

Contrast this with the beginnings of leaderless growth in the decision-support profession, still described incompletely as the accounting profession; it's not working well yet because there is no coherent reason to grow. Each of its specialties carries forward its own separate reason to grow from its twentieth-century Followership origins, along with the durable networks of people that accompanied it. Each individual component purpose, the Followership foundations of its culture, is separate and distinct from every other culture.

For example, accounting continues to be defined by objectivity and precision. The measurement of earnings and assessment of financial position and funds flow still exist as the foundation for opinion giving on audited financial statements. This was the original seat of power, the place of the Giants of their profession.

Quite the opposite of that, far from objectivity and precision, the origins of financial-services culture come from the freewheeling days of stockbrokerage in the 1980s. And just like medicine, the field has evolved considerably since then. Success was once defined by how much money brokers made for clients, but the culture is evolving toward an advisory role that helps clients have a stake in the process as well, evaluating their own risk tolerance and helping them make their best risk-based investment decisions.

Even further distant from accounting culture, many members of technology teams in accounting firms are still smarting from the loss of rock star status they enjoyed in the days when technology followed technology prior to the dot-com bust of 1999. The idea of being employed by an accounting firm still feels like a letdown for some of them from the excitement they all felt when the invention of technology led economic growth. They felt that their work was more relevant to society then.

These new specialties that have been added to traditional accounting firms, and many more, each bring cultural uniqueness that increase the diversity of experience of those firms, but paradoxically also serve to dilute their effectiveness as modern organizations that must now operate as well-oiled, outcome-producing organizations. Many exist as companies with a mixed bag of seemingly unrelated specialties.

Just like medicine, decision support's shift to a leaderless culture will require moving from a profession that hands down purpose to colleagues to one that treats all stakeholders as equal partners in its Followership Agreement. The Days of the Giants are over and, as such, the decision-support profession must begin to reimagine and renegotiate its twenty-first-century reason to grow. Decision support will not grow as a leaderless profession without it.

To illustrate by comparison, imagine an NFL team arriving on the field on Sunday, each player not really knowing why all the other players were there on the field with them. Imagine further that not only did they see one another as irrelevant, they also viewed one another as possible competitors in the greater scheme of winning their own personal game, so much so that each player began playing in his own game on the field, each one with his own idea of what "winning" means. Rather than "Together, We Make Football," we would have "Together We Can Play Ninety-Six Different Games." It is a statement of purpose that would be so confusing that there would be no fans in the stands.

Happily though, the reason to grow of the decision-support profession has quietly, if painfully, arisen out of the ashes of the death of its twentieth-century social-capital foundations. But just as in our emergency room medical example above, there is an emotional loss. These durable networks of people from the prior century, where accounting dominated the decision-support landscape in business, felt like family structures: each member had a place. And each could grow into a tribal leader themselves by first showing respect for the existing social order, and then finding one's own place in it.

A client friend of mine was lamenting the loss of these growth "tribes" to me one day. The social order, and growth that it provided, was coming apart in his business and he was struggling to explain why. He said, "There were *always* spats in the family. But the family *stayed together*." He went on to make the same complaints we hear privately about less loyal clients and less committed employees, especially younger ones. No one seemed to accept their place in the family any longer. Many younger participants seemed to ignore the family structure entirely, insisting on having influence in it that hadn't been "earned" by abiding by the social order provided by its leadership foundation. All my friend could see was the destruction of the social-capital foundation that had fueled growth for his business in the past.

I recall finishing a presentation in New York and having a leader point to the screen where I had drawn a clinical system of practitioner relationships that showed how they might work together in a leaderless model. At the center of the drawing was a person who would be the operational equivalent of today's primary care physician, performing services for patients that would help them integrate all specialist care into a single cohesive plan to deal with his or her health care and maintenance needs—an outcome-producing experience, if you will.

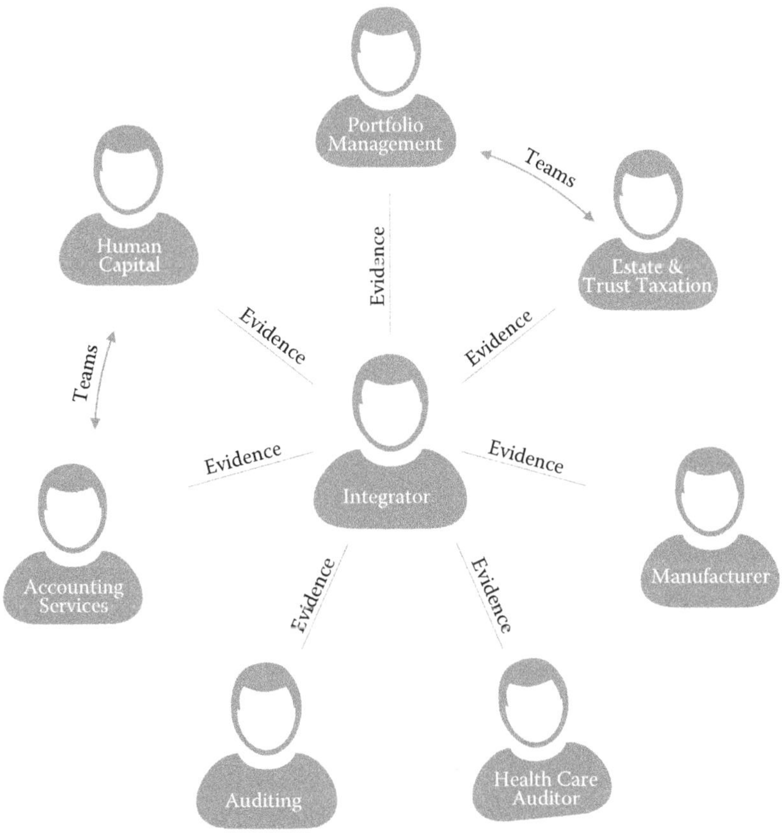

Pointing at the center of the screen, he observed, "We can't find those people." I didn't have a very good answer for him. What he was clearly looking for was someone to occupy the leadership position before the beginnings of leaderless growth. He was looking for that Giant that listened to clients, redefined priorities where necessary, and then led the other specialists by telling them how to modify their plans to account for those changes. Just like my other management friend in the enterprise resource planning engagement above, he too was looking for that elusive leader who would be "in charge" and who "knew what was going on." He didn't realize, and neither did I right at that moment, that at the center of the picture was not a leader, but the equivalent of the telephone operator in our medical leaderless example.

While this shift in the formation of our Followership Agreements promises widespread change toward leaderless growth, one crucial thing stays the same: the needs of people are exactly the same as they have been since recorded time. They are the same for Baby Boomers, Millennials, and any other generational description we will ever describe. And by understanding what those needs are, we can find a way to navigate through Followership change more quickly, and far less painfully, than we have up until now.

There is no evidence that the needs of human beings have changed throughout history. And yet human behavior changes *dramatically* over the course of every new Followership Cycle. Each time a new technology environment is created during the beginning of an industrial regeneration cycle, people become more isolated from one another—in their specialties if you will. When that stress happens, people spontaneously start to adapt by forming social capital that is sufficiently elevated to counter the effects of those newer technologies. This is how people adapt to one another's needs.

People *need* one another to grow. That fact has not changed. And they will absolutely *persist* in responding to that need until they get what they're looking for. But this idea is *directly at odds* with the narrative that casts newer generations as ignoring existing social capital and its institutions. They are thought to be the narcissistic, impatient, self-involved Millennials who can't wait in line for their turn, rather than creators of new, more powerful forms of social capital.

To better understand the needs of people, it helps to look at Abraham Maslow's hierarchy. His description of human needs presented a stackable look at the development of individual people. It starts at the bottom with people's most basic physical needs, draws upward through their need for emotional security through affiliation, and then ends all the way up at the most complex needs for high-level moral development. Implied in all

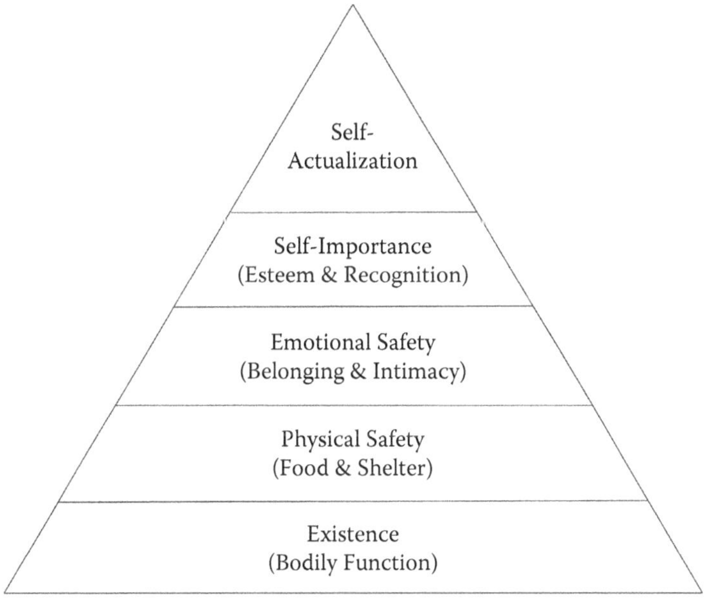

of this, but not discussed, is that people influence one another along their own developmental paths. That is, not only is this theory helpful in thinking about individual psychology; it is quite useful in the study of sociology, the study of group behavior.

Maslow's middle order of needs, those serving people's emotional security needs through affiliation, provided the social capital foundation of our durable networks of people in the twentieth century. The Followership tribes that arose then relied heavily on these needs, emphasizing cooperation in a tribal setting. This tribal social order created persistence of effort, which in turn led to economic growth. And all these tribes needed Giants, the leaders we still want to believe will save us someday, at their forefront to lead their "families" and provide fairly for the growth and security of all tribal members.

But then, as technology began following technology in the mid-1970s, the industrial regeneration process that marked the resetting of the Followership Cycle began. And the construction project of twenty-first-century social capital began so quietly that no one even noticed. The reason we know this is that we can see direct evidence that the social capital built through durable networks of people began to decay through the increased efforts to prop them up with ever-greater employee-engagement efforts and ever-higher-minded mission statements to try to keep everyone motivated to persist. This marked the beginning of the end of the time when tribal security would be an adequate human reward for showing increasing persistence of effort in producing and buying one another's economic contributions, the real source of a rising middle class. People would need better social glue than what their durable networks of people could provide to them.

In Maslow's next order of need, just above those governing emotional security of group participation, lies the recognition of a unique self; and then above that, self-actualization. These levels are not only crucial to the growth of human beings as individuals, but they are now crucial to group persistence of effort in a leaderless environment. If there are no Giants, no tribal leaders, to manage the social mobility of tribal members, people must define *themselves* first as a prelude to finding their unique place—where they "fit"—in the bigger picture of contributing to a great social good and thus *creating their own* social mobility.

So, quite the reverse of being self-absorbed, narcissistic children that are ignoring the family structure of their tribal leaders, young people are showing *exactly* the right human adaptations they need to build twenty-first-century social capital; they're spontaneously responding to their more isolating environments by adapting to the elevated social capital needs of the future, preparing themselves for functioning in a leaderless environment of *shared* purpose by developing strong visions of their unique selves, their *individual* purposes.

So, when my audience member in New York suggested that he "couldn't find the people," it told me he was looking for someone who didn't exist any longer. Not only that—the person that he was looking for, a tribal leader, *wasn't even needed* any longer. He was looking for a doctor who barked orders in the emergency room, not a telephone operator. The conversion to a leaderless model for growth had already begun when he wasn't looking. And far from lacking someone who was "in charge" or who "knew what was going on," the next generations had cleverly stopped making this model of integrator long before it was apparent to the rest of us that they would no longer be needed, or even possible.

The profession of medicine is clearly much further along the social-capital development path than our decision-support profession, or anyone else. Their need for Giants is disappearing. But if medicine no longer needs its leaders to define purpose, negotiate quality, and define accountability, what drives persistence of effort in a leaderless environment? More pointedly, why would people who work in hospitals and clinics keep working there, if no leader exists to help them see their higher purpose? Where instead are they getting it from?

The answer is that medicine is about a half-century ahead of the rest of us in its transition to leaderless growth. Its own path toward specialization began in the late 1970s and continues today. And as medical specialization and its technologies increased the cost of medicine, practice quality became fragmented in the eyes of patients, very much like how clients of what we call the accounting profession feel about us today. The perception of quality, skyrocketing by any objective standard, was plummeting in the eyes of society. Medicine's response was to include patient feelings—their outcomes—as a key aspect of practice quality. But just as critically, they began to invite the patient to account for his own health, asking him to manage risk factors in a way that hadn't been required before.

All this led medicine to fulfill its obligation to society much differently than it had back in the twentieth century. All stakeholders, including the patient, were now equal partners in its leaderless growth environment, to the point that payors are now required to accept the result of doctor and patient cooperative, evidence-based decision-making and the resulting treatment processes.

All these negotiation pressures ultimately defined purpose, negotiated quality, and defined accountability for an entire profession and its stakeholders. It is a perpetual process that is continually refreshed through its living Followership Agreement. And in our current Followership Cycle, it's a template for constructing the global social capital we need to produce the new rising middle class in America.

Professional football has shifted as well. In the 1960s, teams were populated with players who stayed employed by their teams for their entire career. Coaches were colorful characters who motivated their teams with imagery that placed durable networks of people, the team, above all else. It was a time of great leaders, as we like to warmly remember them today. Vince Lombardi's exhortation to his players that their loyalties were to "God, family, and the Green Bay Packers," in that order, very cleverly and effectively steered his players toward one another in common purpose.

Today, the notion of employing those sorts of motivational leadership techniques is laughable. No one could credibly stand before his team and elevate it to near-equal status with God and family. The message would fall completely flat. Compare that *leadership* technique of yesterday to the *management* technique of today's most revered and successful NFL coach, Bill Belichick. His most remembered quote? "Just do your job!" The unspoken reality of that stark difference in message is not just a matter of style. It is a natural outcome of the transition to leaderless growth. It's a shift that has permeated the teams themselves all the way to management of the entire league.

Roger Goodell is the leaderless leader of the NFL. His job is not to define purpose, quality, and accountability for the league, but to defend a purpose jointly created by all its stakeholders: "Together, We Make Football." We see this in many of his decisions; it's why Tom Brady's punishment for "Deflategate" was enforced, instead of swept under the rug. It's also why the prevention of violence against women is now front and center in the league's public messaging. All the league's very public moves to expand its fan base hinge on its leader being the *defender of its Followership Agreement* instead of the sum of its team leaders, its former *tribal definers of purpose.*

So, rather than Robert Kraft wanting to fire him for disciplining Tom Brady, Roger Goodell would more likely be fired for *not* doing so in the context of the twenty-first-century Followership. If Tom Brady, or any other stakeholder, were seen to be exempt from its defining ideals as a *league* instead of a loose band of teams, "Together, We Make Football" would be an empty promise that would hinder rather than promote its growth. Phony social-capital promises are easy for stakeholders to identify as the empty cheerleading that they are.

Our new profession, the decision-support profession, could learn from this. When I look at my colleagues' websites I'll typically see drop-down boxes that demonstrate how many specialties they have. First, there is a list of industries served. Next to that is a list of things they can do in each of those industries. This is certainly important information for any new customer who might visit the site to shop their services, but it is also a painful demonstration of an entire profession's complete lack of a coherent Followership Agreement, its social contract.

Rarely on these sites is there anything even remotely resembling a statement of joint purpose, an active quality negotiation or commitment to accountability among all stakeholders. Accountants are too afraid of their customers and employees—their patients and doctors if you will—to do anything like that. So, they get treated separately, with separate marketing materials for each. First, in our employee marketing materials we talk about how we share their values and are committed to helping them pursue their greater *individual* purposes. Then, in our customer marketing materials, we declare our undying commitment to the customer experience. But the greater social contract of mutual responsibility to a greater shared purpose is mostly absent.

These marketing materials, much like Simon's Grampa at the dinner table, say "yes" to everyone in all their messaging, hoping that all parties will like us better as a result and stay engaged. We do this instead of suggesting that all stakeholders have mutual accountability to a single Followership Agreement—a unified reason to grow—because leaderless commitment requires the vulnerability that comes from treating one another as equals and then following one another to a better, more exalted, place together. If one were to try to craft a statement of purpose that included all the information we see on a typical professional service firm's website today, the message contained in sixteen services provided in six different industries would sound something like, "Together, We Can Do Ninety-Six Different Things."

Today, accounting and its allied goods and services, or decision support, is just beginning to recognize its unified and leaderless purpose of creating outcomes for stakeholders. Regardless of their specialty, there is a growing recognition that all we can really do beyond performing expert tasks such as preparing tax returns, conducting audits, managing investment portfolios, or administering retirement plans is to provide the economy with its best decision-making material. We are not the Giants of the past, who could reassure people about an uncertain future by telling them the business equivalent of "take two aspirin and call me in the morning." Increasingly, the role played by all members of decision support such as accountants, consultants, and professionals in financial services, data, risk, and assurance is to provide information necessary for stakeholders to make decisions for themselves in a world of uncertainty. In pursuit of that emerging reason-to-grow all our efforts are being groomed to focus on relevance, transparency, and choices.

This story of Followership produced by socio-industrial regeneration isn't new. It's happened before and it will happen again. More important than a tale of technology though, this story is a useful tool that tells us a lot about the predictability of human behavior caused by the interplay of two important things: people and capital. Even though the stresses of technology are the *catalysts* for changes in human behavior, the choices made by human beings to deploy capital are what drive the *pace* of those changes.

There is no such thing as human capital; the term is nothing more than a wish that durable networks of people could still produce social capital growth and by extension, economic growth. Social capital, on the other hand, does exist. It is expressed as the growing likelihood of people to persist in joint efforts that pursue common goals. And a look at its historical evolution is useful in helping us understand the nature of it, where it comes from, and how persistence of effort has evolved to meet the needs of each new industrial regeneration. This pursuit is not an intellectual process, but an emotional one. The needs of people for physical security, emotional security, and personal growth must be adequately provided for, or persistence of effort declines and social capital depletes.

A historical look at the Followership Cycle is a tale of highly competitive titans of industry building new infrastructure. At the same time, it is also one of great social upheaval for people and their families. The politics of their times and the evolution of their institutions all formed around this rising economic activity. And durable networks of people created by their Followership Agreements arose out of all of it to create a rising middle class in the twentieth century.

This history now tells us that twenty-first-century Followership Agreements will not use economic transactions to create social capital, as happened during the previous century. Quite the reverse, it tells us that the social capital being built by today's generations will be the *creator* of economic transactions. And this unique historical moment presents them with the opportunity to become the Greatest Generation of all, our New Giants.

Chapter 3

The Followership Story

We've now seen where the current Followership Cycle is taking us: new socio-industrial regeneration is building a leaderless workforce to facilitate the growth of social capital in a more digitally connected, yet less humanly connected, world. But how did we get here, and what's holding people back from following other people to the successful future they all deserve? The answer lies in the history of Followership.

Each regeneration of the socio-industrial cycle called Followership is a story about people. Its different phases only refer to people and technology "following" one another to illustrate how people interact with one another during the invention, assembly, and eventually the full utilization, of any new system of industrial support. During this cycle, wealth is generated differently depending on the phase. First, it is generated by the invention of the raw components of new technology, then wealth is created by reorganization of those components into a new system of support, and finally, growth is led by the productive inclusion of people who then enjoy increased social mobility in the form of a rising middle class each time a new cycle matures. That interplay of people and technology influences people to invest in business organizations, work together inside of them, and purchase one another's efforts in largely predictable patterns.

The first step of the Followership Cycle occurs when **technology follows technology.** This is just another way of saying that some people amass great fortunes by competing with one another to build new technology infrastructure. They "follow" one another by competing vigorously with one another—think Jobs and Gates, vying for dominance in the creation of decentralized computing in the late twentieth century, or Rockefeller and Carnegie building out the oil and steel industries in the nineteenth century before them.

Critically though, these people do so with no defining vision in mind other than defeating a rival and amassing great financial capital in the process; they give almost no consideration to how these new technological advances will affect the people who will produce and use them. They think of their success entirely in terms of the financial capital they grow. During this phase, technology is preoccupied only with itself; Rockefeller sells more oil, Carnegie sells more steel, Gates dominates the operating-system market for the PC, Jobs dominates the design of the PC.

Once all these raw elements are maximized, and the underlying technology elements approach maximum capacity, growth is led by people starting to integrate with a newly forming infrastructure; this is the second phase of the Followership Cycle, when **people follow technology**. The raw components of technology begin to take shape as a single system of industrial support, instead of an unrelated band of newly created elements such as email, cheap oil, microchips, cheap steel, or web pages. All those components start to become something more than just the sum of all their parts.

In this second phase, economic growth is led by people following technology to the places where it has created new jobs. For example, in the late nineteenth century people moved to cities to work in the newly created factories on assembly lines such as those in Detroit at the Ford Motor Company.

This is the phase in which people must learn to fundamentally change the reasons and methods of how and why they work together. And it can be quite tumultuous, as it often demands that people uproot themselves and their families, to abandon a prior way of life. This can create conflict, anger, division, and disengagement. If that sounds familiar, it should—we currently sit in this second phase of the Followership Cycle today as some of us have "moved to Detroit," into cyberspace, and some of us have not.

That disruption has economic ramifications. Change scares people, and scared people are not productive. Because of this, each new attempt to radically alter the integration of people and technology in the workplace must account for the needs of people in profoundly new and different ways. Without these considerations, human productivity breaks down and persistence of effort declines. When this happens, when economic growth from people "moving to Detroit" to fill new jobs taps out, financial capital finally gets around to investing in "people infrastructure"—addressing the new needs of people working inside these newer, more isolating, technologies. That's what takes us into the third phase of Followership, and this is what's starting to happen right now: the needs of people must now be accounted for.

At this point, the third phase of Followership matures into **people following people**. This happens not just through newfound productivity in the workplace, but in an accelerating pattern of consumption of goods and services that a newly productive labor force can now afford to buy. This new social mobility for people leads to a rising middle class. A significantly rising percentage of our population achieves this mobility when all those new tech components finally form into a fully functional infrastructure—*both* a technology *and* a people infrastructure together as one.

Reaching this point sounds straightforward, and in a way, it is: build the tech, wait for people to adapt to it, and address their new needs as they try to do so. But such a dry assessment belies the tortured historical path human beings follow to achieve the fruits of this final phase of socio-industrial development. Just look at today. Even beyond the struggles to adapt to technology up until now, people still face the onset of artificial intelligence and other process design innovations that will disrupt their lives every bit as much as the lives of those who "moved to Detroit" were disrupted over a century earlier. Building a technology infrastructure was the easy part. Building people infrastructure is not. Luckily, we've seen this happen before and can learn from our past.

When Technology Followed Technology

John D. Rockefeller was a dominant and highly competitive person. In the late nineteenth century he saw the opportunity to accomplish what he referred to later as "organizing" the oil business using a set of competitive practices that by today's standards would be judged ruthless and profoundly unethical. Rockefeller utilized techniques such as predatory pricing, secret buyouts, and collusion with the railroads to grow his wealth. Of course, he didn't see it that way; instead, he believed he had a special talent that had been given to him by God and that he was obligated to use it in the way he did.

His actions were not guided by any vision of the coming uses for cheaply refined fossil fuels in America; they were guided by his own pursuit of wealth, his attempt to “win the game” of accumulating wealth. Although he did hire scientists to discover new uses for it, he was not driven by any ultimate purpose for refined oil, such as combining it with steel to form the modern auto industry. He simply assumed there would be a growing need for it, and set about the task of making as much money as he could from refining and selling it. This was, in his mind, ordained by God.

And he was not alone. Other highly competitive industrialists followed his lead. After an earlier career investing in railroads, iron, and petroleum, Andrew Carnegie made his biggest mark in the steel business. Similar to Rockefeller, he was merely responding to a great business opportunity without much regard for the needs of anyone else. He proved it was possible to build bridges out of steel instead of other more expensive materials, thus opening a new market for steel in bridge building.

Neither of these men knew they were creating the raw elements of what would serve together as the technology foundation that would enable a rising middle class in the early twentieth century. To them, it was simply technology following technology: industrialists trying to destroy one another through increasingly ruthless competitive practices and technology innovation, aimed at dominating the growth and development of elements that only later would become a coordinated system of industrial support. People weren’t considered whatsoever.

For example, after Rockefeller had achieved control of over 90% of the oil refining business, he made deals for preferential shipping rates with Cornelius Vanderbilt’s railroads, thus further driving his oil competitors out of business. When Vanderbilt allied himself with a competitor, Rockefeller responded by starting to build pipelines to eliminate oil’s reliance on the rail system. Then, as Andrew Carnegie and a partner began planning for a pipeline of their own, Rockefeller shut down his Pittsburgh refineries to starve his new rivals of business. All these competitive decisions and actions continued as they “followed” one another by attempting to dominate the growth of financial capital.

To them, labor’s only role was to populate jobs they created. The notion of those laborers having needs beyond making wages for work performed was the furthest thing from their minds. People could be counted on to work because they needed to do so to make a living. They needed to feed, shelter, and clothe their families, in line with Maslow’s lowest order of needs. Financial capital of the day provided nothing more than that.

When People Followed Technology

Still, all these technology advancements presented opportunity for people to improve their lives. Wages were much higher in urban factories than they were in low mobility rural economies. Between 1875 and 1900, mass migration to cities began as people moved to the jobs that were being created there; people followed technology. Cheap refined oil, steel, cement, and electricity had formed the foundation for the construction and maintenance of the buildings in which they would live and work, as well as the roads and bridges for them to make the journey there.

This was a time of widespread social unrest. The Gilded Age was a term taken from an 1873 novel by Mark Twain that satirized the "thin gilding" that glossed over the social upheaval and widespread economic inequality of the times. A few capitalists made enormous fortunes building the raw materials of industrial infrastructure, and a small middle class developed among those that supported them. But labor was fractured into a disorganized mass of people who began to blame one another for their plight, not unlike today, as people follow technology into cyberspace.

That social upheaval very naturally flowed into American politics. The presidential election of 1896 paralleled that of 2016, both thematically and in terms of nastiness and anger. That's not a coincidence; the country sat then in a similar place it does now, right in the middle of the uncertain and painful second phase of the Followership Cycle. Then just as now, not only were the new technologies failing to produce a rising middle class, but the underlying forms of social capital that supported two different Followership phases was split between the old and the new.

A bitter election debate about monetary policy masked what was really at the heart of the election: the lack of a rising middle class. One foot of the United States was firmly planted in nineteenth-century social capital, durable networks of people in agrarian, rural America. And the other foot was planted just as firmly in twentieth-century social capital, created by people working in new urban industries. People had started following technology by moving toward these new jobs, but not everyone had begun to follow; this split in the foundations of social capital supporting people became a source of immense social strife.

The political rhetoric revealed the real narrative between our two subsets of durable networks of people. William Jennings Bryan, who opposed Republican William McKinley in that election, was a fiery orator prone to calling out the frustrations of this conflict between the two Followership

Agreements: "Burn down your cities and leave our farms, and your cities will spring up again; but destroy our farms, and grass will grow in the streets of every city in the country." Bryan was unafraid to pit American against American in his populist quest to win the election. He characterized the debate about monetary policy in a purposely divisive manner, and in doing so, he helped to effectively divide the underclass against itself. Not unlike 2016.

There was universal belief among these poor, struggling citizens living on farms and in cities that political and social reform was necessary. Everyone wanted the same thing: a more upwardly mobile middle class. But the debate wasn't initially about their *common need* to share a social contract that would support social-capital growth, a new Followership Agreement; rather, the debate was about the *unique experiences* they lived in their increasingly different transactional lives, and the social capital that those transactions had created.

The political debate in 1895 over the money supply was lively, spirited, and passionate. It was also ultimately pointless. It merely served as a fulcrum over which the struggle between nineteenth-century social capital and twentieth-century social capital could be debated. As such, while often characterized as being about values, morality, and truth, the debate was really about the validation of the transactional lives of people now living in clearly different Followership Cycles. And the best way to galvanize each group was to pit them against one another.

The election of 1896 resulted in the election of William McKinley, not the populist William Jennings Bryant. McKinley had been the candidate supported by the industrialists of the day, and after his first election, business and the pace of social change continued as usual in America. But the underlying social unrest didn't go away.

When People Followed People

It wasn't until McKinley's reelection bid that a new political figure had begun to emerge. Teddy Roosevelt, although a Republican, was mistrusted by his party because of his populist ideas and rhetoric. To render him harmless he was installed as the vice-presidential candidate behind McKinley, and they proceeded to win a landslide victory together. But McKinley's assassination early in this second term elevated Roosevelt to the presidency. That event is considered a crucial moment that marked the beginning of the Progressive Era in American society.

This Progressive Era was a period of great social activism and political reform that lasted into the 1920s and beyond. Roosevelt's attacks on the monopolies and his promotion of consumer protections were merely a small part of a wider movement. All our institutions began to form themselves philosophically around the idea of a greater social good. And the theme of all these efforts was the humanization, modernization, and stability of a society that had been thrown into disarray by new technology's isolating effects on people. People began to follow people—finally taking more direct action to address their needs. And the economy began to rise.

As factories thrived, so did the durable networks of people that populated them. These networks became the foundation of the stabilizing and growing social capital of the twentieth century. The conflict between farm and city, so vehemently debated in the election of 1896, gradually began to disappear as labor productivity took hold to make rising numbers of ordinary Americans full stakeholders in their own economy.

One interpretation of this history states that the political reforms of the Progressive Era caused the rising middle class of the mid-twentieth century. But while activism surely catalyzed political reform and inspired social change, it did not create the social contracts themselves. The Followership phenomenon of people following people, increasing numbers of them producing and buying goods and services in an accelerating manner, is caused by labor productivity alone. And the resulting empowerment of people is what causes political change.

It's easy to see how the political and social dynamics of that time mirror those of today, as people once again try to adapt to modern technology. This time, however, technology doesn't exist in any one place, such as Detroit. It's nowhere and everywhere. Because of its lack of a location, people must follow today's digital and web-based technologies through global sourcing of people, material, and information. So, rather than following it to American cities, people are "moving to Detroit" by following those technologies globally. And it is that global flow of people, information, and materials that presents us with the social upheaval that defines our Second Gilded Age, and the opportunity to grow beyond it.

And just like last time, there is a fulcrum in the political debate today that is symbolic of the struggle between Followership Agreements of two different cycles. This fulcrum once again allows workers in various parts of America to cast one another's beliefs about social capital in terms like morality, values, and truth, thereby pitting themselves against one another. This time, the fulcrum for debate is not the movement of money, as it was in 1896. It is the movement of people: immigration.

It's common knowledge that the free global movement of people is only one component needed to create a global system of accelerating growth. But immigration provides a simple, easily visualized political cause that allows opponents to frame the debate to suit its election needs: as rich versus poor, government versus people, and cities versus middle America or nation versus nation. But immigration is not the real source of people's current discontent. It is the same environment that our country experienced at the beginning of the Progressive Era that led us into the early twentieth century: the combined effects of dehumanizing technologies and increasing disparity in social mobility caused by overlapping Followership Agreements, one ascending and the other descending.

Around 1975, the streak of labor productivity provided by twentieth-century Followership reached its peak and began to slow down. But that decline in labor productivity had nothing to do with the relative efforts of human beings; people weren't working less hard. It was simply that the underlying socio-industrial infrastructure, built of cheap oil, steel, and durable networks of people, had been fully tapped for growth. And the death of twentieth-century social capital began. But, that stagnation in labor productivity was masked by new economic growth caused by the beginning of a new, regenerated technology infrastructure. A new Followership Cycle had just begun: once again, technology began to follow technology.

Renewal of the Cycle

Today, there is similar conflict between the Followership Agreements of our recent centuries. The durable networks of people that assembled around our factories in our less populated areas are grieving the loss of social capital they enjoyed in manufacturing towns. They are no less angry or scared than their ancestors were over a century before at the prospect of losing the social-capital foundation of the lives they built working on their farms.

But it was time for the renewal of our industrial infrastructure. Just as when technology followed technology during the middle of the nineteenth century, great industrialists arose to compete with one another for dominance in the new frontier of decentralized personal computing and global personal connectivity—the Internet. That renewal, its most famous and visible competition for dominance between Bill Gates and Steve Jobs, began in earnest right around 1975. And the changes that these isolating new technologies would have on our economy would start the clock ticking toward the death of twentieth-century social capital, and begin to highlight the need for higher, more effective, forms of it.

People began to detach from one another in the economy—slowly at first. In response, organizations added new elements to their leadership foundations that were intended to increase employee engagement. It was during the 1970s, for example, that the concept of adding "vision" to mission statements gained popularity. During the 1990s came the addition of "values." Despite these persistent efforts by leadership to find a way to deal with this unfolding leadership crisis, employee engagement remained a growing problem.

At the same time, consumers started to detach from the trusted brands that had served as expressions of their economic confidence during the middle of the twentieth century. Brands could no longer maintain customer persistence with silly, aspirational promises. In response, slogans such as, "You'll wonder where the yellow went, when you brush your teeth with Pepsodent!" migrated to "Get your teeth their whitest," as consumer loyalty waned in the face of slowing social mobility. Wages were stagnating, as was worker and consumer enthusiasm for decreasingly effective twentieth-century social capital.

Labor productivity itself became a popular management pastime, as continuous improvement programs gained popularity in the 1980s. Sets of tools emerged to help companies further parse and organize manufacturing processes to extract maximum profitability out of existing industrial technologies. These efforts produced further profits. But in the absence of rising social capital these efficiency experts tended to further alienate and scare employees about the security of their jobs. These measures did nothing to address the now-accelerating disconnection of people from one another—and the growing social unrest associated with it.

Then, as is the fate of all economic bubbles, the growth phase where technology followed technology burst in 1999. Speculation in the marketplace for all things dot-com ceased, and a new reality settled on the economy. Now, the raw components of the new technologies needed to be integrated into a coherent infrastructure, and people needed to be deployed to it. In other words, people needed to follow technology.

Much like the innovators' call in the late 1800s to "move to Detroit," people began to follow technology into an increasingly isolating digital world. But, instead of the mass migration of people to our cities, people followed technology into cyberspace along with all the other inputs of business such as material and information. Everything could now be sourced from anywhere without regard to location.

During this period of economic growth too, just as it is when technology follows technology, financial capital preoccupies itself solely with this movement of the inputs of business—and people are one of those inputs like any other. It continues to ignore the needs of people inside these new, dehumanizing technology environments. And it does so not because of any fundamental lack of consideration by one group of people toward another, but because, as capital, it necessarily follows the path of least resistance. It can do nothing else. During any Followership Cycle when people follow technology, as we see today, financial capital is preoccupied with the integration and efficient use of resources in its technology infrastructure. There is no consideration yet for the need for a "people infrastructure." This process is often quite brutal.

As people flocked to cities at the turn of the twentieth century, no one helped financial capital grow quite like J.P. Morgan. His method of financing, organizing, and scaling the operations of increasingly larger companies became known as "Morganizing" a business. And one of the "resources" available to him was this new influx of urban workers looking for a better life. As competition grew inside each industry, and labor became increasingly plentiful, he responded by lowering wages and increasing the hours of workers. During this time, long and bitter labor strikes dotted industry as labor began to assert itself in response to those types of practices used by Morgan, Henry Frick at the Carnegie Steel Company, and others.

Similarly, now in 2018, as people continue to follow technology into cyberspace, financial capital is not preoccupied with the needs of people. It is focused on the path of least resistance to profits. The "Morganization" of the economy is happening right now. This financing, organizing, and scaling of operations has led to the same human disconnection as the previous Followership Cycle, as the final scraps of profitability are squeezed out of global material, information, and labor sourcing—people following technology.

But, as economic growth stagnates at the end of any period where people follow technology, capital finally must address the needs of people. Not even just because, well, they're people, but because it is no longer profitable to ignore them. As growth from the early Followership phases becomes tapped out, better forms of people process innovation, such as artificial intelligence today, are implemented. But for people productivity to lead economic growth using these technologies, rising forms of social capital enabled by people infrastructure must be built at the same time.

Henry Ford was neither a socialist nor particularly interested in the needs of people as they related to the greater social fabric. He was, however, one of the earliest manufacturers to recognize the true nature of the labor productivity problems in the early twentieth century. He looked at those problems, and the high labor turnover associated with them, as opportunities for investment in people that would pay enormous dividends for his company.

His early methods of investment went straight to the heart of that need for social capital. He created Ford Motor Company's Social Department, an attempt to pay attention to his workers that was considered controversial even in its day as being paternalistic, intrusive, and overreaching. His goal was to reward good social behavior by reinforcing company social standards of behavior through economic reward.

Even though he backed off its most intrusive methods, he still maintained in his 1922 memoir that along with the need to give people social help for "decency's sake," he also stuck by a view that a "broad workable plan of investment and participation will do more to solidify industry and strengthen organization than will any social work on the outside." It was one of the earliest recognitions that it wasn't just that people *should* follow people to be successful. Ford recognized they *needed* to follow one another in their workplaces and their lives.

Beyond assembly line process innovation, his *most important innovation* turned out to be his recognition of the need for rising social capital created by the isolating new technology of a moving assembly line. Ford needed a twentieth-century Followership Agreement. Although he abandoned its most controversial elements, such as using a company "Social Department" to monitor employees' personal lives and financially reward personal behavior, Ford's productivity beliefs began to permeate the company's labor management practices. In a move that stunned the world in 1914, he raised the minimum rate of pay at Ford Motor Company from $2.34 to $5.00 per day, more than doubling most of its workers' pay.

Productivity and profits from this move were immediate and profoundly beneficial for workers. Employees at Ford Motor Company could now afford to buy the products they built. This was unheard of in the days when people followed technology. Consumer goods were largely reserved for the upper classes. And leisure time, once a right of class privilege, became a requirement of that same productivity. Quite the reverse of Morganizing his company by lowering wages and increasing hours, he substantially raised wages and lowered weekly hours to what became the standard in America for generations, the forty-hour workweek.

Interestingly, of all the great industrialists of his time, Ford was the *least* inclined toward philanthropy. While historical contemporaries such as Rockefeller and Carnegie competed to give away the majority of their wealth, Ford was suspicious of charities and regarded work as the sole legitimate means of resource accumulation. As such, it was not a softer, gentler form of capitalism that propelled him to create the defining Followership Agreement of the twentieth century. It was cold, hard analysis and a great intuition about the profound need for people to follow one another that motivated him. His interest in social matters was solely related to their effects on worker productivity.

There is no such recognition by leadership today as we live out the final years of people following technology—now into cyberspace. Wages are rising for skilled workers, but these residents of "New Detroit" are struggling to connect to one another in meaningful ways in our new world of plug-and-play people. We are living in the final death throes of the Followership Agreements of the twentieth century pioneered by Henry Ford. The durable networks of people that he so skillfully organized are simply no longer powerful enough to help people persist in following one another in our technology-connected, but people-disconnected, economy.

Everyone's growth and progress is dependent on successful movement through the Followership Cycle. For example, when **technology followed technology**, accounting firms grew as they helped clients install new, very expensive and proprietary technologies. Software development and rapidly growing processing and storage power leapfrogged over one another, as new titans of industry competed to monopolize the raw materials of a budding new infrastructure. And the accounting profession followed by providing investors and managers with a common set of decision-making information called financial statements. They helped facilitate the growth of financial capital and by association the resulting social capital of durable networks of people that formed around our economic transactions.

As **people followed technology** after 2000, a system of industrial support began to form from those new elements, and people began to follow it. As the race began to find the lowest cost forms of labor, material, and information around the world, the people inside what was starting to become the decision-support profession still followed financial capital in its quest for growth. We expanded specialties to meet the needs of a growing technology infrastructure and then we Morganized them for efficiency, just like everyone else in the economy. But we were still following.

As the newly formed decision-support profession now finishes its own "move to Detroit," it is faced with an environment not unlike the bygone Gilded Age that shadows them on that uncertain journey. The last profits available through people following technology are being reaped and growth has stagnated. And just like most organizations living and working in our newer, more isolating technology infrastructure, decreased employee engagement and customer loyalty are the result of people becoming less relevant to one another. And all of this is unfolding in a global environment of labor unrest, as those who didn't "move to Detroit" struggle to find their place in a world that has left them behind.

It should strike us that a profession whose sole reason for existence throughout history has been to provide a common set of decision-making information for people to use in making their best risk-based decisions should be at the *forefront* of growing social mobility for all its citizens, not merely following technology to the Internet like everyone else. It is decision-making material that helps people and organizations design, execute, and ultimately take responsibility for the experiences that form their economic outcomes and provide for that mobility.

But to serve social mobility for everyone this time, instead of growing common sets of decision-making information for investors and managers to use to support the growth of *financial capital*, this new profession will develop common sets of decision-making information for the holders of *social capital* in the twenty-first century: every man, woman, and child everywhere in the world. And just as it has been during any phase of the Followership Cycle where people follow people, as they most surely will again soon, the people of the decision-support profession will participate. But this time, instead of following the builders of social capital in the global economy, they will lead them.

Chapter 4

Social Mobility

Money can't buy happiness, or so the saying goes. And yet we still must work for money to feed, clothe, and shelter ourselves. There is at least some sort of happiness associated with that. And even being able to buy better, more expensive goods can lead to feelings of an improved life. Eventually, though, the adage holds: buying more stuff stops providing us with increasing levels of satisfaction. After our lower-level needs are taken care of, the foundations of social capital must move up Maslow's hierarchy to serve higher-level needs than mere survival.

In addition to money, most of us pursue work to be with other people. Working alone tends to produce social misfits of all kinds, such as business-book authors, for example. Most people avoid that cruel fate because people need other people to interpret themselves. We need one another not only so that we can buy and sell stuff to one another, but to define our place in the world. Determining the success of our existence in comparison to others is where social mobility is determined. And that mobility is a key part of what drives the Followership phase where people follow people. None of us can exist on an island because we would have no one to whom we could compare ourselves. And yet much of today's technologies threaten to put us each on our own islands, as being next to one another becomes less necessary to work together.

As we just saw, the opposite was true in the twentieth century. Ford's auto assembly lines brought order to workflow. These moving assembly lines reduced production time of a car from twelve hours to about ninety minutes, and because of that efficiency, workers could suddenly afford to buy the very products they produced. This phenomenon produced social mobility as people began to focus on higher level, less immediate needs than their survival. Now, they could envision lives that included pleasure, social affiliation, and recreation, things only available to the upper classes before.

But this new inclusion of people came at a cost. The social isolation of working on an assembly line disrupted people's ability to interact with one another on a regular and continuous basis. Oddly, the very thing that provided higher productivity in one way, such as producing more cars at Ford, ran the risk of lowering productivity at the same time due to the isolating work environment. People no longer had to be near others to do their jobs. Without accounting for that problem with the addition of people infrastructure, there would have been little net improvement in productivity. Physical labor back on the farms may have been more grueling in terms of more hours worked and physical stamina required, but assembly lines introduced new forms of stress that threatened social mobility for reasons other than a simple lack of money.

Social mobility was slow in the U.S. agrarian economy of the nineteenth century because land ownership dominated its Followership Agreements. Becoming a new owner of land was extremely hard to do because systems of land ownership dating back to our European roots systematically protected landowners' rights.

Working on a farm had a strong social cohesion feature though: people were not isolated from one another by technology. The system of social order was clear and consistently communicated to its Followership participants. And because survival was the underlying foundation of their Followership Agreements, strict adherence to the social goal was required. People followed people in a disciplined manner that strengthened their relative relationships with respect to one another. The social capital that formed, while not providing a great deal of social mobility, was very stable.

So, despite how difficult it was to grow beyond the existing social order in agrarian America, the Followership Agreement held in place. Government stood on the sideline as a decider-of-last-resort of the fairness of that system and mediated disputes under a standard of "consent of the governed." As a whole, society accepted some level of inequity so long as social order was maintained, an agrarian economy's Followership Agreement's most important feature.

In what used to be the accounting profession, we hear similar stories today as we reach the end of one Followership Cycle and enter a newer one. Older accountants nostalgically recall hundred-hour workweeks during "tax season," not because they were pleasant but because they produced a more stable form of social capital than that of today, where relatively pampered folks might only be asked to work fifty-five-hour weeks. People bonded over that shared difficult experience. And some still remember it warmly as a place where lifetime bonds were forged with colleagues, not unlike the more stable relationships people had working on low-mobility farms before them.

And while a fifty-five-hour workweek certainly sounds better than one twice as long, that same unrecognized stressor has arisen. Workers are once again experiencing further separation from one another as new technology places each of us on dehumanizing islands, our own isolated spots on a technological assembly line. And just as it happens when leaving any one source of social mobility, people will defend the old Followership Agreements to combat this new isolation, rather than look to higher forms of social capital to provide meaning and mobility in their work and lives.

Just as it is in all parts of the economy, it is the *stability* of our descending social-capital foundation that people will defend fiercely, despite its social *mobility* limitations. The death of any Followership Agreement is met with resistance because it shakes the foundation of the continuous process we've been using to interpret our own position in any given social fabric, even when those social systems start to limit our ability to get ahead in life.

There is a strong historical correlation between rising levels of human need, as illustrated in Maslow's hierarchy, and the rising social mobility provided by new Followership Agreements. In our previous agrarian economy, the only expectation we had from the workplace was that it would provide us with survival. That began to change as land began to be replaced by corporate financial capital as the foundation for new Followership Agreements.

Unlike land ownership, financial capital in its corporate form provided great social mobility for previously excluded Followership participants in agrarian America. Neither John D. Rockefeller nor Andrew Carnegie was born into money, as previous Followership Agreements might have required. They worked, negotiated agreements, borrowed money, and invested it. This relatively newer form of wealth, corporate financial capital, was much more easily accessible than land. It was the foundation of the familiar American mythology of the self-made man.

However, access to this capital and the ability to grow it required a ruthless competitive streak. Although financial capital was universally available to all in theory, only those with the necessary focus, personal-risk tolerance, and competitiveness could possibly survive in such an atmosphere of unknown potential where there were no rules to define the new playing field.

Because of this, people suffered terribly in the early days of late nineteenth-century industrialization. The businesses of these builders of industry earned reputations as places of great suffering and inhumane treatment of workers, due to practices such as seven-day workweeks in physically dangerous environments and child labor practices. But interestingly, the writings of these men reveal none of the wild disregard or hatred that one might expect from a "Robber Baron" who was only interested in his own success and welfare. This is because they were focused on growing a technology infrastructure, not a people infrastructure capable of restoring positive social capital growth. They had plenty of growth opportunity available to them without it.

Far from feeling hatred or disregard for people, they were simply operating under the nineteenth-century Followership Agreements of agrarian life, along with their social mobility expectations. Under those agreements, labor existed to perform work at "fair remuneration." In the previous agrarian social structure, rules were strictly enforced and the notion of upward mobility was completely foreign. They saw no reason to alter what they perceived to be a fundamental truth.

Today, no one could look at those inhumane environments, with children working alongside their parents in factories for up to sixteen-hour days, and assume that they were built by anything less than immoral people. And yet those conditions persisted, long after both Rockefeller and Carnegie were retired or dead. The history of child labor is a story that we cannot lay solely at the feet of early industrialists, but at our own. The practice continued because we were unable to let go of the social structure of a dying Followership Agreement.

The history of child labor law is a revealing study of ourselves and our government. Congress passed successive laws restricting child labor in 1918 and again in 1922. Both were struck down by the Supreme Court. Then, in 1924, the U.S. Congress passed a constitutional amendment prohibiting child labor. Only twenty-eight of the necessary thirty-eight states ratified that amendment. It wasn't until the Fair Labor Standards Act of 1938 that the government, among other things, restricted child labor to the rules we know today.

As much as we would like to cling to a mythology that tells us the Robber Barons were bad guys and we the people, the good guys, rode in on white horses to save the children, the history of Followership tells a different story. Legislative history tells us that when child labor was effectively ended in 1938, it ultimately became law because children were outcompeting their parents as cheap labor.

In short, it wasn't morality that guided the change; it was the realization that our own social mobility as Followership participants would be brought to a standstill if children worked not alongside their parents, but *instead* of them. The entire Followership Agreement and its social mobility proposition would be at risk. All of this was brought on because people were so painfully slow in letting go of the social capital of their previous, low-mobility agrarian lives.

Just like most people living then, J.D. Rockefeller, Andrew Carnegie, and J.P. Morgan were unable to interpret their actions in any way other than the soon-to-be-dying Followership Agreements from which they came. The idea that the workplace should provide emotional satisfaction of any kind would have been thought of as preposterous at the time. Adequate pay was their only perceived obligation to people who worked in their companies.

As outdated and extreme as this sounds, it's not that different than what we see today. Those industrialists who built the technology infrastructure that triggered the growth of twentieth-century social capital were just as mystified about the rising needs of people as many of today's leaders and managers. They have no idea what to do with the new need for personal growth that younger workers are presenting. On its face, it isn't easy to look at a generation of workers that wants reduced hours, greater individual recognition, and more immediate impact on their work environments as being anything much more than the *destroyers* of social capital. But they're actually preparing themselves to be the *builders* of newer, more effective social capital. And we can see how if we look again at Maslow's hierarchy of human need.

When a new Followership Cycle begins, our work environments become more physically isolating. As such, people are less able to interact with one another in a directly responsive manner. Workflow protocols become programmed, and there is sometimes little room to respond to one another beyond what's called for in those protocols. Anyone who has experienced a phone-center call where the service worker is clearly reading a script, rather than listening and responding to you, knows just how unsatisfying this kind of less-than-human encounter can be.

Each time this happens, people spontaneously respond by raising the bar of human needs that each transaction is required to serve. They demand meaning from their work, and by "meaning" we're not referring to some vague notion of 1960s navel-gazing. True meaning is achieved at work through a process that blends self-identity with one's place in a social order. Without this constant process of the merger of self and environment, human beings can't possibly interpret their own social mobility. There is simply no frame of reference to determine our progress without it.

And if this process isn't constantly reinforced through most of our transactions, we as workers, consumers, and other stakeholders begin to detach from joint activity because it doesn't serve our needs. We start searching for meaning elsewhere. And in doing so, we become those supposedly less-loyal customers and less-committed, narcissistic employees who seem intent on destroying the Followership Agreements of our industrial past.

Prior to our seventy-five-year history of uninterrupted labor productivity that lasted from roughly 1900 to 1975, the social capital of life in rural America was grounded in simple survival, Maslow's lowest order of human need. This was enough because of the high-contact human interaction environment. Unlike the participants in our call-center story above, people in a farm work environment communicated regularly and continuously in a face-to-face manner about the purpose, quality, and accountability of their transactions. Those communications provided the constant reinforcement of self and social position that is the requirement of any Followership Agreement.

Once assembly lines started isolating people, workers could no longer negotiate purpose, quality, and accountability in a face-to-face manner. They began seeking higher forms of human need to make up for the loss of that frame of reference, the *meaning* of their work. For example, just above the human needs for physical survival—food, clothing, and shelter—Maslow described the need for people to be affiliated with one another. It was these needs that began filtering in to the workplace where they had been nonexistent before. Emotional security became a socioeconomic requirement as our institutions began to make it a priority in the ways they managed labor, created brands, and defined social priorities.

Today, as people become even more physically isolated from one another because of the Internet and globally operated businesses, the current social-capital environment is once again completely inadequate to meet the needs of people. Just as the Followership Agreements of agrarian America died because of new technology, those of the twentieth century are dying because of it too. And just like the last time a set of Followership Agreements died, there is something much better ahead for us, because we are climbing even higher in Maslow's hierarchy once again to better serve one another's needs for meaningful lives.

That higher level is based in the definition of self. It's marked by the developmental needs of self-esteem, recognition, and importance, and it's these needs our new generations are seeking. Intuitively, it's hard for us to think of these "selfish" needs as being elevated over the need for group security; people need to serve other people, and recognition of self over group needs doesn't seem to agree with that socially focused goal. But this attempt to better understand ourselves as unique individuals prepares us to attempt to achieve the highest level of human development possible: self-actualization.

Self-actualization, the ultimate goal of social mobility, is the merger of self and relative position to others. It is the stage of human development where we are capable of serving others without fearing for ourselves. Prior to this stage, we use the concepts of self and position to serve our own social-mobility needs, but self-actualizing people are preparing themselves to help others with theirs. In this light, younger generations are far from selfish because, by paying closer attention to themselves, they are better preparing themselves to serve the needs of others using their best talents and skills.

Abraham Maslow described the attributes of human beings that begin to approach self-actualization. It is at the top of the human-needs hierarchy, and he estimated that only one in one hundred people could ever achieve it. It is exactly this aspirational quality of striving for self-actualization that makes its pursuit sustainable. It is a worthy goal to permanently pursue even though so few of us will ever completely achieve it. He recited the qualities marking that level of human development as a lack of prejudice, true morality, and acceptance of fact.

Taken in the context of society today, these attributes are the exact opposite of what we see playing out. Both sides of the social-capital argument accuse one another of using false ideologies to promote hatred with fake news and groundless opinions about government policy. Many of our citizens worry about the loss of the transactional lives of their work, and the relationships that once formed around those transactions. Their social mobility is in a downward spiral away from the emotional security of twentieth century; it looks to them as though they are headed back to the nineteenth century. The combined portrait of self and social position looks grim to them.

Living life inside a dying Followership Agreement is painful. And its members can easily be misunderstood by those who have already begun the journey to the next one and the social mobility it provides. A profound wish to return to one's economic past is really a desperate longing to return to a place of comfort and belonging with others; people want to follow people.

And when their system of doing so goes into decline, they are very unhappy about it. The resulting argument is then conducted in the same painfully familiar ways each time rising forms of social capital threaten old ones: William Jennings Bryan's campaign rhetoric about "destroying our farms" over a century ago or "Make America Great Again" today are poignant examples of the wish to restore our past forms of social mobility.

This phenomenon is why elections in between Followership Cycles are marked by a divided underclass, when only some people are successfully following new technology and its resulting new social capital, and others are holding tight to the past. If these types of elections were merely about money, work, and fair treatment of people, those living below the middle-class watermark would unite against the "moneyed class."

But they don't rise up against financial capital, because they are not arguing entirely about money. They are defending the depleting reserves of the social capital of their lives—the durability of their networks of people. These networks are how they interpret themselves and their place in the world. And intuitively, they know that twentieth-century Followership Agreements and their transactions cannot exist without businesses to create them. So, when the underclass defends financial capital, it is really defending its dwindling social capital reserves, sometimes long after that defense isn't in their own best interest.

As these citizens descend into the fear that is created by worrying about having to live their remaining lives without the social mobility that their past gave them, they become incapable of thinking objectively and nonjudgmentally about the situation, or of making truly moral choices in pursuit of the best interests of themselves and others equally—as a self-actualizing person might do. Instead, we have a whole lot of ordinary people "debating" in the absence of any real information through name-calling and accusations of immorality and lying. And there doesn't seem to be a solution other than to wait until the new Followership Agreements take over from the old ones, allowing the social, economic, and political landscape to stabilize.

This Darwin-like assessment that the Followership Cycle progresses at its own pace suggests that we are powerless to do anything about it, that we must simply let it play itself out. But we know after looking at it more closely that the speed of an underlying technology isn't what drives change during a Followership Cycle. It only catalyzes it. The needs of people are only met once they adapt to the stresses of their new technology environments. This adaptation, and by extension helping to accelerate the formation of the new Followership Agreements of a new century, always requires the selfless courage of new generations of people ready to help.

Prior social capital flew on the wings of transactions created by business. And decisions to deploy financial capital were made by relatively few leaders, in the days before leaderless growth. We know that financial capital will look to the quickest return, that it will take the path of least resistance. Thus, it only pursues the real productivity of people after it taps out the growth available through building and deploying new technology infrastructure. In recent history, the entire socio-industrial regeneration called Followership took about 125 years. It was the behavior of financial capital's decision-makers that limited the speed of the cycle, not the speed of the technologies underlying it.

We worry today about how people might fit in a future artificial-intelligence economy. And we know that being able to afford consumer goods is no longer a ticket to economic inclusion, as it was in the twentieth century. Consumer goods can now be produced so cheaply and in so automated a fashion that they're useless as the social-capital generator we so desperately need for people to lead economic growth. Between this and fears of about automation, the future can look dark and intimidating.

This colors how we talk and think about global growth. Commentators on the subject almost universally talk about growth in terms of the "next big thing" in technology. But we know from a cursory look at previous Followership Cycles that after the fundamental components of new infrastructure are in place, growth from further building of it will slow. Today, for example, consumer technology has been reduced to relying on Fitbits and smart watches to provide new growth, far cries from founding elements such as personal computers and cell phones. GDP growth from the creation of the elements of infrastructure has been largely tapped out.

Today, economic growth is focused on people following technology. For example, Amazon, using modern computer technology combined with cheap oil, can deliver almost anything to anyone globally at a fraction of prior costs. Computer-assisted means of transporting people more efficiently, such as Uber, popped up seemingly out of nowhere to bleed some of the last few scraps of efficiency out of the more regulated environment of local taxi services. And global labor sourcing through cloud technologies allows people to follow technology to and from anywhere that fiber optic cable exists.

But our adaptive future as people is still out in front of us, and with it, the true definition of this current Followership Cycle. Sometimes we refer to this future economic growth as being the "information economy."

What we call "information" is an interesting case study in semantics and how our beliefs can change quickly. I recall being told in my early accounting education that data was not information because it hadn't been parsed, analyzed, and regurgitated in a manner that produced a conclusion. Information was the result of the digestion of data. Today though, instantaneously produced data is information in and of itself.

As such, it is only useful to think about information if we consider its actual use. Information is what we use to make decisions, and if people are going to follow people again, this is a crucial point. We are not really entering the age of an *information economy,* but the age of the *decision economy.* So, while technology certainly changed how we think about the definition of information, the far more important thing it has taught us is that we need to make decisions much faster than we used to.

We need much better outcome-producing decision material at both business and consumer levels. As Henry Ford taught us so long ago, a rising middle class cannot exist if the labor force cannot afford its own products and services; that's how everyone becomes truly included in an economy. As a result, we know that Followership Agreements of the new decision economy must deal with the inclusion of every citizen too, or they will fail to produce a cohesive society.

To the people who already adapted to technology in the early twenty-first century, achieving some degree of social mobility seems obvious. Adopt technology, get an education, and move where the work is, instead of staying where social capital and the transactional world that supported it is dying. Unfortunately, human behavior doesn't work that way. Social progress moves very slowly because some people adapt to new foundations of social capital early, and some adapt late.

The folks who will follow you into your new century will need help getting there. And in turn, you will need their help constructing the new Followership Agreements of your time. That's because real social progress can only be achieved when everyone has equal access and is *included.* And that equal access becomes more realistically possible each time a newer, more universally accessible way of generating social capital arrives.

In agrarian times, land was virtually unattainable unless you already had some. Financial capital was slightly more accessible, but you had to fit a personal profile of risk tolerance and competitive spirit to successfully grow it. But the social capital of the decision economy, in its purest form, is available to anyone with Internet access; it's far more accessible and mobile than land or financial capital. And just as financial capital devoured land as the primary form of wealth generation, this new social capital will devour financial capital for the same reason.

As such, the Followership Agreements of the twenty-first century won't be dependent on slow-moving financial capital for its transactions. That form of Followership construction was dependent on the assembly and maintenance of durable networks of people, which have become too slow to serve the growth needs of people or organizations. But joint persistence in the pursuit of a higher purpose, the role our new generations are preparing themselves for by defining their unique capabilities, will have much greater potential for growth. The construction of *this* form of social capital doesn't rely on financial capital to produce it. Quite the opposite, purpose-driven social capital will be the creator of economic activity.

But the change is off to a rocky start, as is typical when the social capital of one Followership Cycle is being eclipsed by the next. These conversations are difficult, just as they were in 1896, and probably no different than they will be in the election of 2136.

What used to be the accounting profession has suffered a lack of growth for the same reasons as much of the rest of the global economy: it has been unable to leave its past tribal growth methods. Fewer and fewer young professionals are interested in the inclusion offers from firms, not because they aren't interested in money, but because inclusion in those old Followership Agreements doesn't provide the meaning that it used to. They no longer provide an adequate way for people to define themselves and find their place in the larger world.

Many leaders today are just as mystified by this as Rockefeller and Carnegie were in their own time about how and why people's behaviors change in newer workplaces. Knitting together a cohesive, leaderless decision-support profession has been difficult. Newer forms of decision-making material arise constantly. And each time one does, the practitioners who specialize in older forms fear the loss of importance of their own specialty. Accountants feel eclipsed by data that is used to make decisions before they can form opinions on it, to the point that some are even predicting CPAs will become obsolete in the not-too-distant future.

It's a fear held by people across a variety of industries; how do people stay relevant to one another when their duties are changing so fast? The answer lies in finding new forms of stability to replace the declining stability of durable networks of people. If people can no longer be counted on to remain in one place forever, then the only way for them to remain connected in a system of social mobility is to make their *purpose* permanent, their reason to grow.

Contrary to popular belief, *society doesn't need more truth.* Finding the truth and giving it to others is nothing less than an attempt to rob them of the opportunity to find it for themselves. In the new decision economy, what society will value the most is better decision-making information for each member of the Followership Agreement to *draw its own conclusions about the truth.* This is the heart of Followership in the twenty-first century. It's how everyone can be included, and it will be the key way people with roles in the decision-support profession will stay relevant to one another and society.

Acceptance of fact, lack of prejudice, and true morality. This pursuit of relevance, transparency, and choices will be your reason to grow, as well as the foundation for growth and social mobility for everyone in the world.

Chapter 5

Unique and Meaningful

I once heard a journalist describe the research method for a book he was writing. As with many of our best authors, journalists enter each new field completely uninformed about a topic and then make it their business to find out the "real story" underlying the subject matter. He mentioned that an advisor had once wisely told him to "find out what they're afraid of, and you'll have your story." The story for us today, even among those of us who have "moved to Detroit," is that people fear losing the comforting things they're familiar with. We cling to some of the remnants of our durable networks of people despite their decreasing social mobility rewards and are suspicious of specialization, process automation, and leaderless growth, despite their spectacular growth potential for people and organizations.

Without proper people infrastructure in place, process automation does have the potential to make us feel even more irrelevant and interchangeable in the decision economy than we already do. Current estimates tell us that nearly 40 percent of all of today's jobs will be automated over the next twenty years. It's counterintuitive to think that people now desperate for group meaning should think about letting go of the very thing that provided it in the workplace before: a secure social structure that continually reaffirmed our position inside tribal growth "families."

An acquaintance of mine read my first book, in which I wrote about growing limitations of the decision-making powers of professional service providers, and how in the past, that power was what made them Giants. I didn't have the example of our leaderless emergency room handy then to explain what I really meant to say. He felt the language I used was disempowering to professionals by suggesting the trend toward decreasing leeway for individual practitioner decisions. To him, it raised the specter of a dystopian future with human beings living their lives in subservience to machines. His felt that if we automated decision-making, we would become interchangeable servants of those machines.

He especially bristled at the notion that professional judgment would be limited or automated in the name of *efficiency*, proudly proclaiming himself to be more in favor of *effectiveness*. It seemed to him that the power to make decisions was at the very heart of any profession, and that any attempt to take away that power would be dehumanizing to professional service workers, especially if it were to be done in the name of moving a process "assembly line" faster, which he assumed to be the whole point of efficiency.

In the emotional noise of the conversation, I was unable to convince him that effectiveness and efficiency are not opposing concepts, but rather the numerator and denominator in one single quality equation. And I was also not able to get through to him that automating certain human decision-making in the workplace is one of the keys to a future of meaningful, empowering work, facilitating personal growth for all stakeholders—not just the Giants.

In the new decision economy, meaning will come in the form of activity that assists the decision making of *users* of information, not the decisions of the *producers* of it. Taken in that light, as robots take over our knowledge management duties they will be doing us a big favor: they will handle less meaningful decision-making related to information assembly and expertise deployment, so that we can concentrate our actions on helping the people we serve with their more meaningful outcome-producing decisions.

There is nothing magical about human beings' ability to adapt to meet their own need for meaning at work. The more that process automation reduces human interactions, the more we seek to make the remaining interactions more meaningful. As such, the secret to real productivity in the decision economy is coded into the needs of people and not into the isolating technology that created those needs.

Just as I failed in convincing my acquaintance, I also failed even in trying to explain this to my own daughter. Anne is brutally direct in knocking me off my intellectual high horse (named Pontificate, if you must know) and laying out what I need to do to communicate my ideas to people. She said, "You're telling people that they're going to lose all this really good stuff (twentieth-century social capital), then go through some really hard stuff (process automation), all for some new really good stuff they can't really picture, somewhere in the distant future (twenty-first-century social capital)." She didn't seem to think that scaring people by talking about what they were going to lose was a great way to start trying to lead them to a better future.

My author friend and my daughter are just like everyone else in the economy today. We all want the warm glow of the familiar, and the emotional security we felt living in our durable networks of people in the consumer economy. We want this for very understandable reasons. This Followership environment served as the foundation of prosperity for nearly a century, as the emotional security of the consumption economy provided meaning in our lives. In contrast, when asked about their jobs today, many young people shrug and say things such as, "It's a job." It's not a place that defines their unique self and provides meaning in a world of other people; it's just a job.

But you wouldn't know it by reading most companies' content marketing and stakeholder-inclusion statements. Testimonials from ecstatic employees and customers assure us that we're all at the top of our fields in engagement and loyalty. But despite these cheerleading marketing efforts, the majority of today's young employees and consumers feel irrelevant and interchangeable. In today's workplace and consumer world, they rely on small scraps of relevance and meaning left over from the consumption economy to get by, and its remnants of outdated interpretations of concepts such as team, trust, and relationships.

So, it's entirely reasonable that no one would want to think about their jobs in a way that scared and depressed them first. People wouldn't be able to get past the scary stuff, the stage where their familiar forms of social capital begin to fall away or the stage where human work place decision-making is replaced by robots. And yet the scary stuff is all we see in news stories as they follow the advice of our earlier reporter to "find out what they're scared of" as the foundation of a story.

Fortunately for us today we get to write the rest of that unfinished story, not as newspaper reporters but as professionals who are collectively bound by duty to serve the public interest in a fearless, objective, and morally inclusive manner. And the key to finishing the story of how that one profession, on the brink of disappearing into irrelevance, helped sow the seeds for twenty-first-century social capital, is to start by getting a good handle on its *reason to grow*, the foundation of our new Followership Agreements. Without that, we'll have nothing to pursue together and will be stuck worrying about the twentieth-century social capital that we'll be leaving behind. All we would see ahead of us is loss.

We've seen this slow lag in social capital regeneration before. We always worry too much about the past, and it always slows us down from getting to the new good stuff more quickly. Think, for example, of the children who migrated from occupying a unique and meaningful role in agrarian life to one of irrelevance and interchangeability in an industrial economy. Work situations that would be considered starkly immoral by today's standards were not considered to be so in the beginning days of the twentieth century; people just did what they were used to doing.

In agrarian life, the work that children performed was considered preparation for an adult role in subsistence farming. Every member was highly relevant to the family economy, each learning unique roles that contributed to the meaningfulness of a greater shared accomplishment. While today, we wouldn't view that as sufficient reason for children not getting an education, this system was critical preparation for children's futures. Farm families' cohesion as a social unit was assured in this arrangement as they built homes for their children in nearby fields, so that they could help with cooperative farming and elder care. No one foresaw that the coming shift to factory life would shatter this role children played in the social system.

Yes, they were still "specialists" in their new industrial lives. For example, they were smaller than adults and could maneuver into tight spaces to repair and clean machinery. And they had smaller and more nimble hands that were better suited for certain work than adult-sized hands. But the work that they did was no longer in preparation for a larger role as an adult, nor were they able to view their efforts in the wider context of a functioning family farm, a socioeconomic unit.

All that they could see was their specific role in producing an industrial product. They were now irrelevant and interchangeable in the workplace, along with the parents who brought them there. They would serve the needs of financial capital until they were no longer able, instead of growing into a larger contributor in a growing socioeconomic unit that would provide context and meaning for their efforts, as would have been the case on the farm.

We know that the story ultimately resolved itself. Children were finally relieved of working in factories. And the Henry Fords of the world brought a level of social attention to the workplace that brought group meaning to what were increasingly dehumanizing workplaces. These social-capital adaptations didn't just find their way into business in the form of company brands and philosophies that emphasized mutual emotional security through consumption.

All our institutions that defined social priorities during the twentieth century—governments, fraternal organizations, churches, and marriages—all followed suit to adapt. Today, in the face of even further automation and isolation, our institutions must respond again. But this time it will take more than consumption to overcome the current social capital decline.

Considering the magnitude of the efforts and accomplishments of Carnegie, Rockefeller, Vanderbilt, and Morgan, we might be tempted to define the social capital that followed as being the *industrial economy*. But industry had already existed before then. What didn't exist was the consumption of consumer goods on a mass scale, which didn't happen until modern assembly-line process innovations and people infrastructure were added to cheap oil and steel. As a direct result, it was the *consumption economy* that defined the twentieth century, *not the industrial economy*. That productivity was made possible by people adapting to the isolation of technology—not *by* technology, but *in spite of it*. Ordinary people in the economy defined the shared purpose and the reason to grow of that Followership Cycle, not the great industrialists of the day or their technologies.

The combination of all those human adaptations together gave people the key to the unique and meaningful existences they needed to produce a rising middle class. Prior to being able to afford the cars they produced on Ford's assembly lines, workers produced them solely for the upper class, then returned home to their subsistence livings. Now, they could aspire to the trappings of life that had looked unattainable before. The resulting social mobility of people was the transformative moment of the twentieth-century Followership Cycle.

Similarly today, there is a painful lag in new social capital development as people follow technology into cyberspace. Just as the children and adults that moved from our farms to our factories struggled with lost social definition, so too are we struggling with adaptation to a newer, more isolating workplace. Once again, automation and isolation is testing people's ability to live unique and meaningful lives.

In the Days of the Giants, work performed by young professionals was considered preparation for one of the ultimate roles as the great definers of purpose, quality, and accountability, as partners. Every member was highly relevant to the team economy, each learning unique roles that contributed to the meaningfulness of a shared tribal accomplishment. The maintenance of those human networks was assured in this arrangement, as new partners built their own practices in nearby offices to help with cooperative labor-sharing and partner retirements. But just like when children lost their roles on the farm over a hundred years ago, we're currently struggling to think about young professionals' lives in the same way.

Yes, they are valued employee-specialists living in their new cyber lives. More technology is helping them produce a lot more information much faster than ever before, so the unit cost of employing them is going down. But the work they do is no longer in preparation for a larger role as a Giant. Just like medicine, the spontaneous onset of a leaderless reason-to-grow has rendered obsolete their role as definer of purpose.

All that many of these young people can see today is their specific role in producing a technical product, not unlike early factory workers felt. They feel irrelevant and interchangeable in the workplace along with the leaders who brought them there. Most of them will serve the needs of financial capital until they are no longer able and then they will leave, instead of growing into a larger contributor in a socioeconomic unit that will provide context and meaning for their efforts.

Fortunately for them, just as it happened over a century ago, the defining and transformative moment of Followership has finally arrived. It's now time to provide people with the tools they will need to become full stakeholders in the economy. Just as in the prior century, the defining reason to grow will spring from the adaptations of people, not from the isolating effects of the technology that made it necessary. As one of the isolated specialists in our firms, Anne knew instinctively about the power and importance of describing this positive outcome to people. She knew that we should talk first about the powerful new social capital that will define the decision economy through helping others shape the outcomes that define their lives.

It is this inclusive pursuit of personal growth for all Followership stakeholders that is the reason to grow of the twenty-first-century decision economy. And the social capital created by pursuing it is at the core of meaningful *work* in our jobs and meaningful *lives* in our communities. Not coincidentally, it is also the foundation of wealth generation in the twenty-first century. Just as the previous century was defined by something people could *do* together—consume—the new century's reason to grow is not technology, information, or the assurance of Giants, but the *decisions* of ordinary people.

That future is under construction now. We can see it in the leadership of our global companies as they each search for their own reasons to grow to serve as the foundation of social capital that will give them a competitive advantage in the market place. It is Apple leading personal privacy and

Walmart leading sustainability. As people will have the opportunity to live increasingly unique and meaningful lives in the decision economy, companies will continue to adapt to their needs. And in the process, they will achieve their own desired organizational outcomes.

The twentieth century convinced us that workers and customers should reflect company cultures and brands as a way of fostering growth and inclusion. This suited the consumption economy's need to have purpose defined for it to serve as the foundation for rallying tribal support. We need to get over this in the decision economy. I once spoke with a young colleague about the cultural challenges of working in his firm. The firm's leadership believed employees were struggling to live up to the cultural aspects of its organizing statements of mission, vision, and values. In his opinion, management's order of "live what we preach" fell on deaf ears because culture is something that "just is." His organization's wish that its employees would proactively promote the "firm culture"—leader-defined purpose, if you will—was at odds with the reality that the organization was beginning to look like the sum of all its imperfect employees and customers.

This crowdsourcing of purpose can make individuals seem narcissistic and social-capital growth unmanageably chaotic. But it is the only empowered response to dehumanizing automation capable of moving us forward as a society. It is the growth of a more highly evolved social capital required by people to find meaning together in a less connected workplace. People need to follow other people. And if they can no longer do so with static, leader-defined purpose inside shared physical space working on an assembly line, they will do so with dynamic forms of leaderless shared purpose in cyberspace. It is this process that creates true organizational culture, not company marketing or baseless inclusion claims.

Accounting, a profession historically responsible for decision support, is ironically struggling in this new decision economy. It has always served the public interest by being accountable to the decision-making needs of those people who created and grew wealth. That source of wealth generation used to be financial capital. As such, accountants could easily fulfill that responsibility by serving a relatively small group of people in business: stockholders, company management, bankers, the government. We produced and examined the measurements of financial capital through auditing, tax preparation and planning, financial services, and, more recently, through the construction and maintenance of the technology infrastructure that facilitated that work.

These activities emphasized *results for shareholders.* That was how wealth was built. Financial capital parsed and regulated its transactions among companies with tools such as scope of work, unit productivity metrics, and measuring deliverables. It adapted only grudgingly to the social-mobility needs of people, much like the early twentieth-century industrialists only grudgingly adapted to the needs of people in their Followership Cycle. The needs of people for meaningful lives were taken care of in their durable networks of people, where uniqueness of self and relative social position grew spontaneously out of the transactions of business.

But now, what used to be the accounting profession is a much broader decision-support profession. It still serves the public interest by being accountable to the decision-making needs of the people who create and maintain wealth. But now, because social capital is becoming the primary generator of wealth, that responsibility to facilitate decision-making of stakeholders extends directly to every human being in the global economy.

As such, it is now the measurement of how well people share purpose with one another—people following people—that will be the most relevant indicator of future growth potential and the ability to manage risk. To respond to the winds of change in that amorphous and evolving mass of intelligence that forms twenty-first-century social capital, organizations will need to have the same adaptive skills as human beings in their quest to stay relevant to their stakeholders. Brand promises and mission statements won't work anymore. Employees and customers don't follow companies today because of what they say in their internal or external marketing. People follow companies because of what people say to one another.

Decision-support professionals will help people and organizations build unique and meaningful lives by facilitating *outcomes for human beings.* This is what will beat back the effects of isolation: people pursuing their common need to live unique and meaningful lives. And this is how wealth will be built in the decision economy. As automation more quickly overtakes certain human actions, we will more quickly begin to form transactions around permanently evolving sets of social principles. As such, the social mobility needs of all people will no longer be the accidental byproduct of economic transactions. They will be the very reason that economic transactions will occur at all.

As Maslow suggested of self-actualization, the idea that decision-making should lack prejudice and be accepting of fact seems very much in line with the needs of society today. It's also very much in line with accounting's historical roots of protecting the public interest by providing useful decision-making materials. But Maslow's most telling statement was his assertion that true morality would guide the actions of self-actualizing people. As is so often the case when we feel like our way of life is threatened, people want to codify and make sacred the transactions of our lives. They inform our beliefs and become a narrow, individual moral view that we think of as permanent. History shows us that it never is.

When leaders fail to help us include others in our beliefs about the common good, we lose the ability to see the needs of others as the same as our own, and we declare those people to be immoral. Without CEOs—or presidents for that matter—who defend this crowdsourced building of shared purpose, global growth fails. We fail.

As such, true morality in the growth of the global economy is best expressed in the permanent crowdsourcing of the truth as best as we can all jointly know it. It is inclusive, not only in its outreach to people of other nations, religions, and cultures, but in its outreach and tolerance of those who haven't yet "moved to Detroit"—those who still believe their meaningful lives can be returned to them with the manufacturing jobs of the consumption economy. We need those people, and they need us. Without them we will never achieve the greater goal of creating the inclusive social mobility that comes from having a rising middle class.

That is the mission, *the relevance*, of the decision-support profession in the twenty-first-century decision economy. The meaning of inclusion in that economy is grounded in relevance, transparency, and choices so that every stakeholder in the economy has an equal chance to live a life of true morality at the pinnacle of human development. Anything less than that will be viewed in the twenty-second century in the same way child labor is viewed today: at best, backward; at worst, immoral.

Chapter 6

Equality

As automation continues to further isolate us from one another, we know now that the only possible way to create rising social capital today is to give everyone an equal voice in the formation of a reason to grow, to put everyone in a position to pursue the personal growth of self-actualization. This inclusive response to the needs of people is easier to understand now that we know why our Giant leaders had to leave us. But despite being leaderless, people still need to find a way to come together to respond to the dehumanization of technology. They need to lead themselves into the twenty-first-century decision economy using concepts such as trust, team, and relationship in ways that are very different than what occurred during the Days of the Giants.

The highly competitive Giant leaders of the twentieth century came to be revered as the Greatest Generation for their selfless service to the needs of others, particularly during World War II. By comparison, narratives such as these have an unspoken "truth" underlying them: newer generations are somehow less than them because they have been unable to produce competitive leaders who serve the social-mobility needs of others. Instead, they seem to be producing what appear to be generations of leaderless and self-involved people.

Competition exists in nearly every aspect of our economic and personal lives. People sometimes compete to improve their own prospects for social mobility over others. But now we know, though, that social mobility cannot happen at all through simple expression of the self. People need constant reinforcement of their position relative to others to have a frame of reference for their own success. Without one another, our social and economic selves don't even exist. So, unlike how it worked for the Greatest Generation, when competition serves only the interests of competitors—and not everyone equally—social capital does not grow as it happened then. It is seriously damaged.

John D. Rockefeller probably ended his life as something less than a fully self-actualizing person. It's a guess we can make based on the contents of his autobiography, *Random Reminiscences of Men and Events*. In it, he does little more than relate just how correct he turned out to be about everything during his lifetime.

Most telling of all was his admission that he'd love to be young and do it all over again the exact same way, including the practices that we think of as immoral today. It was fun building the biggest business anthill around at the time, and to sit at its top. And he believed his personal anthill served an important purpose—he'd organized the oil-refining business in the United States of America. He got to define his own personal reason to grow.

In a self-actualizing state, human beings move beyond their own importance to recognize the importance of other human beings. And they exhibit a form of true morality by beginning to view the needs of other human beings as equally as important as their own, without judging them. And they make their own decisions accordingly—with equal respect for the needs of everyone, putting competition aside for the greater good. Rockefeller's Darwinian approach to winning the game he had created for himself showed nothing like this form of morality. He was entirely focused on himself.

While he was not openly disrespectful of the needs of other people, and didn't appear to feel hatred or disgust toward them, he simply did not view them as his *equal*. Survival of the fittest put him in his natural position as the king of the hill. He didn't view his efforts as rising on the lowliness of others, but as rising due to the superiority of his own talents and efforts.

This is the same narrative we hear still today, in the Days of the Giants. Growth in professional service firms, and the economy in general, was commanded by Giants. These people were the highly competitive definers of purpose who had few equals. They rose to the top because they were dominant people; by extension, their powerful roles as definers of purpose were rightfully theirs.

As a person who had arrived at a level of human development just below self-actualization, Rockefeller was preoccupied with his own self-importance and consumed by individualism. As we've seen, such a charge is also leveled at our younger generations. And yet, unlike Rockefeller, they don't seem to want to defeat one another as rivals like he did. Young people may often look like Rockefeller—individuals consumed with importance and status—but they don't have the competitive spirit we so often associate with economic growth.

Instead, our leaderless new generations seem preoccupied with wanting to cooperate with one another to create and pursue a shared reason-to-grow where everyone is responsible for its construction, accountable to its maintenance, and has equal access to its benefits. They are preparing for a time when *everyone* wins the game, not just the John D. Rockefellers of the world. Instead of technology following technology in brutal competition, these people seem to want to follow one another in cooperation. That shift from competition to cooperation is crucial and fundamental to the final progression of any Followership Cycle to the final phase where people follow people.

Sometimes we more ordinary humans feel privately guilty that we aren't always very competitive. It's a universal jealousy–guilt response we have when we hear the narrative that tells us success only happens when people compete for it. This is illustrated in the never-ending hand-wringing about the much-maligned "participation trophy." We all know it by heart: if everyone receives a trophy, then receiving one becomes meaningless, because trophies should be for winners, not losers. But even just framing the conversation like this reveals something we all tend to believe without much thought: regardless of how they get chosen, winners and losers do, and should, exist.

So of course this *equality* thing has us scratching our leadership heads. Rockefeller, Carnegie, Jobs, and Gates didn't need participation trophies to feel good about themselves. The Giants of medicine and other professional services certainly didn't need constant reassurance of fairness, equality, and meaning to foster group persistence of effort. They defined purpose themselves and then went about enlisting others in joint effort.

Competition versus cooperation lies at the heart of the tension between the two Followership Cycles that are overlapping today: how should purpose be defined, and who is worthy of defining it? This tension exists in current workplaces all over the country. As an example, a young professional told me a story once about an unpopular department leader in his office. This partner's client size and revenue base were larger than everyone else's, so he was promoted to leadership. In days gone by, someone with a very large client following was also a great definer of purpose. He *had* to be, or he wouldn't have been able to provide for the social mobility of others whom he enlisted to help him serve his tribally defined reasons to grow. Client loyalty and employee commitment hinged on that purpose.

This partner was in the habit of walking into a room where his colleagues would be consulting with the office partner in charge, and addressing that leader without even acknowledging that others were in the room. Common courtesy would suggest he wait his turn, but when his large clients had needs, this young man just couldn't help himself. To those around him, his junior colleagues, this looked like he was asserting his status over them. He was demonstrating that they were not his *equal.*

That perception of him may not have been wrong, but in truth, the primary emotion this person was experiencing was competitive fear, not superiority over his colleagues. It's always been true that when client representatives call with needs, it can be a fearsome experience. When a client calls you with a need, they are defining what quality means to them. Immediately then, it is up to someone to marry purpose—a reason-to-grow—with an outside definition of success in pursuing it—quality. They don't always match up, and there's the rub.

Historically, when this happened to the Giants of our profession, they responded by going directly to tribal members to rally support for the client's quality definition. Some sort of negotiation would then take place. We had things such as billing rates that were used by those tribal leaders to buffer this reconciliation of purpose and quality. These billing rates allowed the leader to flexibly manage accountability of everyone toward a purpose he'd defined, pursuing quality defined by a client.

This arrangement provided happier, more loyal clients because someone who was "in charge," who "knew what was going on," could respond to them in a timely, direct manner, just like the general practitioner of that bygone age of medicine, even if his answer was little more than the business equivalent of "take two aspirin and call me in the morning." But the real prize in the arrangement was the fact that everyone's social mobility was provided for. Everyone in the tribe had access to the social capital of these transactions if they played by the rules of the game. It didn't matter that someone was above them in the hierarchy because the system met their growth needs as well.

But this form of social mobility stopped working due to specialization and the "Morganizing" of our products and services. Production lines no longer allowed people to create social capital together in their work, as they had before when they could freely negotiate purpose, quality, and accountability through regular and continuous human contact. Now, it was all about getting each job done as quickly and expertly as possible, with minimal distractions caused by people and their social capital needs.

Firms still wanted increasing revenue. But now they also wanted fewer staff distractions and for everyone to stay in their professional service specialties, doing more of the specific thing they knew best instead of getting distracted by people outside their specialties. The human bonds that made it useful for some people to be "in charge" of others on the team were being destroyed, one engagement at a time.

An early retiree I know put the hardening of the battle lines between leader-defined purpose and consumer-defined quality, and the human toll that it took, as follows: "The firm wanted one thing. And the clients wanted something else. If it was just one or the other, I could have managed it. But it wasn't. It was the pressure between the two that got to be intolerable."

In our young leader's case, too, he was functioning in a world of highly specialized labor that could no longer respond to those purpose and quality negotiations easily. Not only were his human resources more specialized, they were also very tightly scheduled in their specialties. It just isn't that easy any longer to get help with that negotiation between purpose and quality because the tribes have broken down. So, he went right to the office partner-in-charge to assert status over his colleagues, because he was no longer able to lead them like a Giant—in a way that benefited all of them. And suddenly, the glaring inequality of rank and hierarchy mattered very much.

Today, instead of client-service partners providing for the social-capital needs of everyone through negotiation of purpose, quality, and accountability, we are reduced to colleagues appearing to assert their status over one another. And this is happening in a workplace of increasing equality expectations. Specialization has taken that older, tribal form of social-capital generation away from us. In the context of Followership Agreements of the Giants, this lack of equality and assertion of status was simply viewed as an irritating but unavoidable byproduct of team hierarchies. It was a management problem easily monitored and solved with leadership.

But now, in the context of *twenty-first-century social capital,* this inequality is far more than an irritant to group cohesion. It is deadly to the outcome-producing needs of people and the organizations in which they serve. In this leaderless environment, keeping people engaged requires powerful "participation trophies" in the form of equal access to, and accountability for, the reason to grow. Purpose can't just be handed down by leaders anymore. Being nice to one another would certainly be helpful, but it misses the real point—equal inclusion in a shared reason to grow is far more important than simple collegiality.

As we approach the Followership phase that will create a new rising middle class, competition and individual status-seeking are giving way to cooperation and equality. Take another example: a management acquaintance of mine once spoke about a younger partner who was buying him out of his practice. This younger partner was highly competitive, incredibly smart, and voraciously hardworking. And he was successful at building a practice for *himself* because of these qualities. In ranking his young partner's capabilities, and those of the followers behind him, my acquaintance said, "He's a ten. Hell, he's *more* than a ten. But all he's got behind him are fours, fives, and sixes."

This belief that competitiveness, intelligence, and long hours would translate into growth is hardly revolutionary. It worked for John. D. Rockefeller and it worked for my friend's young partner. But somewhere along the way, even though it still worked as a means for his young successor to achieve *personal growth*, it stopped working as a leadership technique for *group growth* for that person's own successors. But rather than question the social-capital foundation, the Followership Agreement, my acquaintance questioned the quality of his successor's young colleagues. In his thinking, group growth should continue to spring out of individual, competition-based growth because it always had before.

But successful group growth can no longer happen as a simple collection of a bunch of separate tribal purposes, like it used to. Leaderless growth requires one cohesive reason to grow, one that has been agreed to by an entire society. Every stakeholder in whatever city, state, industry, or nation who wants to tap into it is welcome to do so. All they need to do is abide by its principles and be held accountable to it to enjoy its growth benefits. No competition required.

These new cooperative Followership Agreements require capital to grow just as any foundation for wealth generation before it. Capital in all its forms has historically provided access to economic activity, which creates social mobility for all Followership participants. This is how wealth is created, accumulated, and invested. But as we've seen, financial capital today is proving too slow and hard to access to provide adequate social mobility for people. But not everyone is quite aware of it yet. That's why my management friend believed his highly competitive, hardworking, and smart successor should have more highly mobile successors behind him. His successor had amassed financial capital through hard work, and was now trying to use that financial capital to generate more transactions, which would allow someone just like him to build even more of it. It was the very definition of growth in the twentieth century. But that time has passed for good.

Similarly, people in the nineteenth century mistakenly believed land ownership would always dominate Followership Agreements by creating a strong system of respect for its ownership and then providing minimally for the social mobility of people. Of course, Rockefeller and Carnegie proved them wrong. It was access to the *newer* form of wealth-generating capital that would dominate the new twentieth century. And the previously inaccessible land would become easily available to them as a result.

Today, we believe the same thing about financial capital in business. It is the thing to pursue and compete for if you want to get ahead in life. And we believe if we strongly respect its ownership and regulate its transfer, and then provide minimally for the basic needs of people, it will stand forever as the permanent gateway to the acquisition of wealth. And just like 125 years ago, we are dead wrong. Not only will social capital no longer be the casual result of the investment of financial capital, the tables are already turning and social capital is beginning to devour financial capital, just as financial capital began to surpass land as the primary form of capital and wealth generation during the Followership transition before it.

This is because social capital is no longer composed of actual durable networks of people, those permanent socioeconomic groups who produce, play, live, and purchase repeatedly over the course of a lifetime. Financial capital could create this older form of social capital by increasing the number of transactions: produce and sell more goods, create more durable networks of customers and employees, repeat. Competition thrived, its potentially negative effects mitigated by the fact that our need for affiliation with one another was satisfied through the personal and economic transactions of our daily lives.

But social capital isn't transactional anymore. Specialization has taken our durable networks away along with the competitive leaders who sought to serve others as a matter of leadership duty. Social capital must instead form around crowdsourced, joint purpose rather than Giants. And it must do so as a cooperative effort—among equals.

We know from history of repeated periods of social order and unrest that new organic growth can only occur through the introduction of more accessible forms of capital. True social mobility for all, and the cohesive society that goes with it, can only be achieved through increasing access to wealth generation. It is the new "fairness" in a world of true global social mobility. In order to take one more step toward true universal access, financial capital is giving way to social capital that is being built through shared, crowdsourced, reasons to grow.

The rising middle class of the twentieth century was not caused by simple production and consumption of goods; it was built through the social behavior of people inside and around those consumption transactions—the cohesive behavior of people happened in *spite* of the efficiency of manufacturing process innovations. And we know that, if we don't pay close attention, our twenty-first-century move toward artificial intelligence will deplete what little social capital is left over from the consumption economy that created it.

In this future world where our consumer products are produced nearly exclusively by machines, decisions about why those products exist and how they'll be used will still be made by people. That can never be delegated to technology. And we will all need the help of other human beings to access decision-making information that is unbiased, factual, and morally inclusive, as Abraham Maslow has taught us. Well beyond finding emotional security in the production and consumption of consumer goods, people in the decision economy will find new ways to create value among themselves in pursuit of personal growth.

We know now that looking to technology to provide us with that rising value is misguided. Technology alone doesn't change anything in a Followership Cycle. It merely catalyzes changes in the *reasons* that people follow one another to create value and provide for one another's social mobility. The days of global growth funded by technology following technology are done for this Followership Cycle. The basic infrastructure is already here, and there is a limit to how much benefit can be achieved by simply speeding up existing economic activity of the previous Followership Cycle, as we see today while people follow technology through global sourcing.

Unlike the robots that are reportedly coming to replace us, human beings can experience something called empathy. It is the ability to understand, interpret, and act upon the feelings of others and to support them that differentiates us from robots. Often, we human beings are propelled through the world around us by fear and desire, not our higher angels. It's no wonder that competition, trying to "win" against each other, is such an ingrained value in our personal and economic lives. People sometimes have a hard time responding to their world in a way that accounts not only for their own social mobility needs, like my acquaintance's successful and hardworking successor, but the social mobility needs of everyone. But this is exactly what is happening with the onset of twenty-first-century Followership Agreements that are forming the basis for people following people to the decision economy.

This crowdsourced and cooperative decision-making economy will be created and led now by our new generations. Just as in the early 1900s, we are perched unsteadily at the transition from one Followership Agreement to the next. At this moment, when many people still firmly believe the comfort, stability, and inclusion of the consumption economy can be returned to them from overseas in the form of manufacturing jobs, this transition will require these noncompetitive traits of our newer generations—empathy, inclusion, and cooperation—to create Followership in the coming century.

And even more so than the economy in general, those of us in the decision-support profession still resist defining ourselves in a more positive and useful way. Just like everyone else, we can now see the end of human involvement in large portions of business decision-making as robots and computer algorithms take over more roles that used to belong to us. We are worried about an unpleasant future where we all exist on the islands of our virtual assembly lines, separated from one another with nothing to do but look at our cell phones and drink coffee at Starbucks.

Instead, this should be cause for celebration, renewal, and recommitment, as opposed to hand-wringing, worry, and avoidance. It is the human capacity for empathy that tells the very real and positive story of a future we should want—and must *start planning for* to remain relevant and useful to our other Followership stakeholders.

The mythology of wealth creation by competitive, risk-taking entrepreneurs using financial capital is ingrained in our culture so deeply that it's hard to look past it to the real reasons wealth has always been created. Sustainably growing wealth has always ultimately happened because people followed people, whether in durable networks or shared purpose environments, people persisting together in rising patterns of production, distribution, and consumption.

All that the captains of industry have ever done, or can possibly do in the future, is help put people in position to follow one another in these patterns of rising activity. And, as the activities of our machinery and robots continue to produce more commodities, it is the efforts of people that will be valued the most highly as we learn to better assist one another in building the outcomes that define our lives.

That once-positive competitive culture led by the Giants of the Greatest Generation was preoccupied with *results* for customers. Under pressure from one another to produce these results in business-to-business dealings, people devised management techniques that defined expected results, contained cost of investment, measured ROI, defined scope-of-work, and set deliverables and price. Unfortunately, all these techniques are designed to mediate the exchange of financial capital in the pursuit of forms of certainty that no longer exist, in the now-futile hope that social capital will somehow magically materialize in the wake of those transactions. Results do not deal productively with risk any longer with the decision economy. However, social capital created by shared, crowdsourced purpose will help people better cope with risk through the formation of something called outcomes.

An *outcome* is a stream of individual results that form a complete human or organizational experience. Unlike results and deliverables that only pursue a specific or narrow goal, outcomes continually pursue a reason to grow. They are formed through the pursuit of something that can never really be attained, becoming sustainable by their very permanence. Another feature of shared purpose is how it continually reconciles self and society—the only real source of social mobility. Results and outcomes can vary widely, and many times they don't fit our own individual perceptions of success. And this reconciliation of quality is crucial to social capital formation today.

For example, Anne called me once to tell me a story of a great result she'd had at work that day. While preparing a tax return, she'd discovered a tax timing difference in her client's favor in the amount of $1.6 million. This would amount to a tax deferral of nearly three-quarters of a million dollars that no one had noticed before her. After her colleagues analyzed it with some skepticism they determined she was correct. She was a proud young accountant to have achieved such a fantastic result.

But separately, the *outcome* experienced by Anne's client, a CFO, might have been quite the opposite. Finding out at tax preparation time that she had an additional planning error of that size may well have disturbed other decisions she had made during the year leading up to that positive tax result. Her *decisions* would likely have been influenced by the knowledge if she'd had it earlier in the year. Finding $1.6 million was a good individual result, though it may well have been a potentially bad outcome.

The reverse can also be true, as was the case with my wife Colleen's experience with cancer. Her result was known from the moment we entered the hospital emergency room. She would die soon. But in the meantime, Colleen wanted to live life as she always had: Get up and go to work, visit with her daughter and new grandson, tolerate her husband as she had for nearly forty years. Despite the inevitable result, her death, there was an outcome to be had in the stream of activities and decisions during the following eight-and-a-half months before she died.

We spent those months living that outcome together as our medical team guided Colleen through what became increasingly limited choices. Finally, the day came in our medical oncologist's office when we learned there would be no more chemotherapy prescribed to combat the cancer. Colleen sat thoughtfully considering the finality of that message, her head slightly bowed.

After a moment, she raised her head and said, "You know, the treatment that we decided on led to a good eight months. We did good." In the face of what she could have characterized as a terrible result, she chose to think of it as a successful stream of experiences, her outcome, facilitated by her best choices as described by the oncology team. Her oncologist and I looked at one another and knew there was nothing to add. The successful outcome was hers alone to judge.

Pursuing this type of organizational and consumer outcome is what will lead growth in the decision economy as people begin to follow people again. And your role as its leaderless leader will be to assist people not just with the measurement of financial capital, but increasingly by facilitating the building, measurement, and growth of social capital in an uncertain world hungry for positive outcomes to replace results that are no longer predictable.

People—employees and customers, CEOs for that matter—live in a world of fear and want. And now, the only way left for us to drive that fear and desire out of the economy is to set aside our competitive, tribal tendencies so we can help lead everyone to a better place together. The social capital that will be created by the decision economy will provide the ultimate tool for social mobility—the ability to define ourselves and our place in the world. Without the decision-support profession leading those efforts toward equal access to social capital, inclusion will remain the meaningless buzzword that it is today.

So, far from a dystopian universe of technology-induced disconnectedness, the decision economy is a place of equal access and accountability to a leaderless reason to grow. It is a place of equality where no one carries anyone's water. We will all be Giants *and* telephone operators. And yes, equal access means we will all get participation trophies.

Chapter 7

Sustainable Impermanence

The change happening to the foundations of social capital presents special challenges that will be difficult for organizations to navigate. It will be even harder for ordinary people to deal with them because it is no longer possible for them to create Followership Agreements all by themselves. So, what can people actually *do* to smooth the transition? As the permanence of our durable networks of people slip away from us, what form of permanence will make growth sustainable? A good place to start is to rethink the concept of permanence at work.

I recall having a conversation with a partner–colleague about employee turnover. It was about ten years ago—back in the day when we still believed that the permanence of human relationships was the key to firm growth. As the office leader, I felt responsible for our growing inability to retain employees much longer than the initial two years they would need to qualify for their certification as CPAs. People were more frequently leaving as soon as they could, and it was beginning to strike me that maybe we were going about things the wrong way. I casually tossed out an idea.

"Maybe instead of trying to keep people, we should concentrate on dealing more effectively with the fact that they're not going to stay?"

A flash of intense anger crossed his face. He was mad at me for uttering such nonsense. To him, I was abdicating my responsibility as a leader.

Our ability to keep employees, "attract and retain" as we used to call it, wasn't a very rewarding occupation in 2006. In hindsight, it's clear the onset of specialization had begun to render our young professional colleagues irrelevant to one another, and interchangeable in their jobs. One way they adapted to that interchangeability was by simply going to the highest bidder for their services. The second way was to leave employment in professional service firms for the world of private industry, where diverse careers in decision-support services were still creating social mobility that professional service firms no longer could.

Trying to keep employees is even less fun now over a decade later, and we've seen why: specialization has taken inter-practitioner and social irrelevance to an entirely new level. And to top it off, young professionals now have easy access to social media to serve their tribal, human relevance needs. So, their need to seek relationship permanence in the workplace declines more with each passing year.

The arrival of artificial intelligence will exponentially speed up this impermanence. The talent acquisition business is having a field day feeding on this reality, as we all compete to purchase relationships we hope will be more durable than the ones before them. We're just hoping to acquire talent that will magically become permanent again at some future date. It's not working because pursuing permanence by saying yes to employees all the time, treating Millennials like they're impatient grandchildren wanting a positive response to their demands, is chasing the wrong thing.

During the Followership Agreements of the late twentieth century, productivity and management experts Edward Deming and Peter Drucker made famous comments about "driving fear out of the workplace" as a precondition to leading a healthy and growing organization. What those comments assumed, and it was true when they made them, is that an emotionally secure workforce is a stable and engaged workforce. Those comments couldn't have foreseen the need for the rise of leaderless growth and its new implications for the rising social capital needs of people during this new transition.

Now we know the social-capital foundations of security and belonging aren't enough to sustain customer loyalty or employee engagement in the new decision economy; technology-based processes have pushed people's social-mobility needs up Maslow's hierarchy to account for the greater isolation. Today, rather than chasing permanence by *driving fear from the workplace*, the new mandate will be to *drive courage into the workplace* through the defense of permanent, leaderless shared purpose. As a direct result, the CEOs of tomorrow will no longer be the great definers of purpose of our recent past, but the great defenders of stakeholder purpose—their reason to grow.

Trying to maintain permanence through networks of people is not only inadvisable as a strategy; it would be suicidal to attempt in the face of the arrival of artificial intelligence. We're told by some estimates today that

40 percent of today's work will be replaced by robots and other automation methods in the coming twenty years. The level of workplace isolation we are about to experience has no historical parallel in its sheer volume. But its effects on people in the economy will still follow the pattern we've seen before. So, if we have that historical blueprint, how can we use it to help us as all transition more effectively to the decision economy?

Today's leadership and management has already responded to this transition by first addressing questions of scale and efficiency, just as J.P. Morgan did in the Followership Cycle predating the consumption economy. Since the early 2000s, workplace software has become far less proprietary and easy to use. Paperless production systems, and the attendant process systemization in tax and audit production, led to great efficiencies of scale.

All these management efforts continued to lower the permanence of people—clients and colleagues—such that it began to threaten sustainable growth. Growth doesn't like impermanence. This forced us to begin managing knowledge because we could no longer expect durable networks of people to retain knowledge for us. With this increased efficiency came more business. Companies grew by increasing their capacity to manage more existing transactions. But social capital was still depleting as people-impermanence accelerated.

In addition to this, growth via merger in professional service firms has taken hold in much the same way that it did in medicine in the 1980s, and the same way that J.P. Morgan used mergers and acquisitions to consolidate operations for the sake of efficiency during the last Followership Cycle in the late nineteenth century. Now that technology has allowed us to routinize and speed up the production of our core products, it makes perfect financial sense to bring in more tax returns and audits, because we all have the capacity to handle a higher volume of work.

In a very real way, this progress in efficiency has worsened the coming challenges. All these efforts aimed at scaling operations, in effect making them bigger and faster, have led to a population of workers and clients that feel increasingly irrelevant and interchangeable. Their work has become part of a uniform routine that most firms have down to a science. It is this "science" of technology efficiency that has effectively become our reason to grow—with appalling social capital results. Technology has temporarily become the Followership foundation that we're asking people to unite around to replace the tribal reasons to grow of the Giants. It hasn't worked yet, and it won't work in the future.

So, the fact that we are about to become exponentially even *more* isolated in the relatively near future doesn't seem to bode well for sustainable growth based on human workplace permanence. And no talent acquisition industry or human capital function can possibly save us from that fate. For growth to happen in that isolated future, the needs of people must be accounted for by making each remaining human transaction even more meaningful, dealing with the elevating social-capital needs of people under increasing technology stress. Scale and efficiency, while necessary, only serves to make the potential social capital need even greater still.

Today, we're doing the same thing J.P. Morgan did over a century ago. Just like him, we are attempting to scale operations and merge our way to the future while still trying to reproduce human permanence as the key to worker engagement and customer loyalty. We treat employees as workers who are entitled to market compensation all the while abiding by Edward Deming and Peter Drucker's advice to "drive fear out of the workplace" by saying yes to them all the time, the Followership standard established during the previous Followership Cycle.

But in neither case, J.P. Morgan scaling business nor us streamlining production to cope with impermanence today, did society create a rising middle class. In retrospect, it couldn't possibly have happened through Morganization, then or now. His techniques treated the needs of people in the economy as though they hadn't changed during the transition from their agrarian lives to their industrial lives. Our current approach is in many ways equally blind to the elevating social capital needs of people.

During the last Followership Cycle, it was Henry Ford who brought real labor productivity to the workplace to create a rising middle class because he was the first to have all the tools at his disposal that he would need to complete the twentieth-century Followership Cycle. Cheap steel, refined oil, a labor force in place in Detroit, and recent discoveries in assembly line technology put him in position to turn auto manufacturing, something that had been a hobby for the wealthy, into an economic engine that marked the beginning of the consumption economy.

Henry Ford aggressively automated the manufacturing process more than anyone had done before. But he also added something new: to counteract the negative effects that automation would have on his workplace, he became a student of human social need and used what he learned to build the structure and operation of his business. It became the foundation of modern management and leadership philosophy that we still use today, albeit in newer, more sophisticated ways.

He is famously quoted as saying, "Coming together is the beginning. Keeping together is progress. Working together is success." He was right then and still is today. And in updating his advice to account for today's even more isolating workplace, we can take the next evolutionary step toward a more morally inclusive and socially mobile society—the inevitable final result of socio-industrial regeneration—as people begin to follow people. His three-step leadership process was really a lesson in Followership, and a lesson in how we can find sustainability despite the impermanence of technology and Morganization today. Ford didn't bring people together to follow *him*. He brought them together to *follow one another* in a rising pattern of economic growth fueled by their own productivity.

And this time around it will be you, our new leaderless generations, leading others to follow one another to a better future by using human impermanence to create newer and more effective forms of purpose permanence. And the operational and leadership programming for how you will accomplish this is coded into the history of Followership.

Each distinct historical phase of socio-industrial regeneration, Followership, requires very different talents and skills and varying degrees of competition, cooperation, and specialization, and uses different forms of capital to create important new sources of social mobility. Today is unique, and advice surrounding it should specifically fit this moment in history. As you develop your plan to embrace impermanence by systematically building the Followership Agreement of your profession, history gives you not just a template but also important guidance on what *not* to do at the dawn of the decision economy of the twenty-first century.

We know now not to resist automation but to embrace it as the gift that it truly is. As frightening as change can be, new forms of social capital arising from adaptations to workplace isolation have always ultimately elevated the interests of workers, both skilled and unskilled. Easing the burden of repetitive work is always a part of the completion of the Followership Cycle. This is why scaling, efficiency, and automation are necessary parts of preparing people to follow one another, despite not being enough on their own. Positive change always eventually occurs with the overlay of people infrastructure on a management and technology base.

But life on the way to that positive change is brutal because of the clash of mismatched and competing forms of social capital. At any given point in history, people define industrial morality through the lens of their daily economic lives; as such, it is truly impossible for all of us to believe the same things about morality at the same time because of the unique experiences we each carry. People interpret the world in wildly different ways, especially at the unique flash point of the change from one Followership Cycle to the next, which we are experiencing today.

As individual citizens, we are free to make moral judgments as we conduct our daily lives just as rightly as anyone else in society. Increasingly, we all shop and create transactions with one another in a manner that is very conscious of companies' reasons to grow, real or perceived. That is a defining trait of the decision economy, and it amounts to the direct social negotiation of morality. That is the right and duty of every citizen in a free and morally inclusive society and it is your right too.

But when you are working in the decision-support profession in the decision economy, you will be duty-bound *not* to participate in these negotiations. It will never be your professional job to define that morality for others, or to assure the public about its positive development. Instead, you will put everyone in an equally informed position to conduct their daily lives in a manner that, collectively, defines morality on an ongoing basis through its transactions.

In the consumption economy, where financial transactions created social capital, your job was to be the independent financial referee in the room, making sure that business played by the same measurement rules. That was what financial capital stakeholders, mostly investors and managers, needed to make their decisions. It was only *after* business transactions occurred that society had a chance to weigh in collectively on the morality of those transactions.

But in the decision economy, where social capital is the *generator* of financial transactions, your job will decreasingly be to referee for financial capital interests. Increasingly, you will facilitate all stakeholders' ability to create morality for themselves, collectively over time through their working, buying, and consuming habits. In the decision economy, society will be deciding morality *in advance of*, and as a necessary foundation to, business growth. And to do that, they need information that is accepting of unbiased fact. This facilitates true, inclusive moral development of a society that needs the input of all its citizens to move forward together.

Albert Einstein is quoted as saying, "The fate of humanity is entirely dependent upon its moral development." As such, our moral fabric today will just as surely produce moral revulsion a century from now about some of today's social practices and beliefs, just as child labor appears immoral to us today even though it didn't then. And that is because the moral development of a society is part of a never-ending process of socio-industrial regeneration that produces a more moral and inclusive social fabric each time the cycle completes. Perfection is never attainable. It is exactly this unattainability that makes its pursuit *permanent*, and thus *sustainable*.

Taken to its logical conclusion, if growth in the economy is dependent on the collective moral development of its citizens, then the fate of humanity is entirely dependent on access to capital, not as an "ism," but as a social-mobility generator that puts every one of us in position to collectively define that morality as equals. That is the true goal of people following people in a Followership Agreement. It's also the true purpose of the decision-support profession in the coming century: supporting people so they can persist in producing, buying, and selling goods and services that pursue the Followership Agreement. But, unlike the consumption economy where economic growth was fueled by the pursuit of possessions, the decision economy will grow because it defines the *meaning* of those possessions.

Supporting people as they pursue purpose together is trickier than it sounds. One of the most destructive things you could do is use your professional position to attempt to educate people about the moral superiority of newer forms of social capital. People don't like being talked down to. They don't like being shamed, ridiculed, or preached at. The key to social moral development is simple inclusion. The only way people will come to embrace the social capital of the decision economy is in their ability to contribute their voice to its creation, and then *experience* its benefits, not to be lectured about their current decisions and beliefs.

Development of a truly moral society requires us to *collectively* accept unbiased fact as the basis for economic agreement. The decision-support profession is positioned unlike any other institution in the world to fill that social capital need in the global economy. You will bring relevance, transparency, and choices to all stakeholders in the decision economy by using all the tools at your disposal: data, risk, accounting, probability, and knowledge assimilation. You will not teach, persuade, or assure any longer. You will simply support other people by giving them clear and equal access to the foundations of social capital. Doing otherwise would destroy your credibility as unbiased, inclusive—truly moral—providers of fact.

It has always been this way. Look at history. During the movement of manufacturing from our largest cities to our rural areas, it was not anyone's job to educate the populace there about the superiority of the social capital of the consumption economy. It was to provide decision-making information to the owners of financial capital about the economic viability of that migration. Analysis of real estate, local laws, and estimated costs helped financial capital plan those operational moves. As financial capital spread manufacturing across the country, the resulting social capital of the consumption economy spread from our cities to our rural areas.

Although it was the social activism of the Progressive Era that helped catalyze improvements in quality of life in America, it was the migration of financial capital from cities outward to lesser populated areas, facilitated by access to decision-making information, that caused the consumption economy and the Progressive Era to happen at all. Without the accounting profession's support, this positive response to the negative effects of modernization couldn't have reached national social and political momentum. It was not anyone's job to preach then, and it isn't your job today. Your job is to serve the decision-making needs of the builders of wealth-generating capital—this time around, social capital.

Today, the builders of social capital are not the owners of financial capital, as was the case in the consumption economy and before that time. Today, the builders of that collective morality are all people making economic decisions. That collective moral force builds every day as people decide whether to shop at Walmart because of perceptions of its efforts, or lack of them, in community building or sustainability. Or whether to buy an iPhone or a Samsung cell phone based on our personal privacy beliefs. Or whether we can support NFL football depending on its ability to positively influence players' social behavior.

And because developing social capital through reasons to grow is a cooperative venture, we should resist the temptation to compete with one another too aggressively. Your colleagues in other specialties such as artificial intelligence, data, engineering, risk, and fraud are not only relevant to you as coworkers, but they are relevant to your own needs as citizens in the decision economy. Excessive competition makes the development of a unified reason to grow impossible because of the mistrust that it fuels.

Imagine if you went into a medical clinic today and felt that the specialist doctors were suspicious of one another's influence with leadership, or appeared to be asserting status over one another, or competed for compensation with one another. You wouldn't be very happy as a patient there, and you certainly wouldn't trust the people whose job it was to support you as you made decisions about your own health. Followership in an inclusive decision economy requires cooperation, unlike the competition that was necessary among our tribal Giants who created the social mobility of the consumption economy.

It's clear now that our response to impermanence can no longer be to insist on assuring people about what is no longer possible, but to start trying to help them make decisions in the more realistic world of impermanence. The idea of being able to assess the past as a way of predicting the future, all the while ignoring what happened yesterday because we're not too sure what it means, will no longer serve the decision-making needs of a population hungry for choices they can use to better their own futures. What we once viewed as expertise will soon be automated through artificial intelligence. And most of us will migrate to the far more rewarding duties of helping other people make their own best decisions.

And to serve the needs of everyone in the economy equally, we need to start letting go of the notion of independence as a viable foundation for enforcing ethical behavior in our work. It was always impractical for accountants to remain independent from an auditee; they were being paid by them, after all. But at least it was arguable that competitors of our clients could gain some comfort in the notion that there was an appointed referee in the system of competing financial-capital interests, whose job it was to make sure the holders of that financial capital played fair with one another using similar measurement rules.

Now that growth will be generated by social capital and not financial capital, we will no longer be accountable only to investors, managers, and a few boards of directors of a few large companies. Our clients will be, directly and indirectly, everyone in the United States, and, increasingly, everyone in the world. There is no way to remain independent of everyone. Instead of independence, providing equal access to information through complete transparency will level the playing field for all Followership members.

Just like the Followership environment Henry Ford faced, you are the first generation to have all the tools necessary to create the Followership Agreements of your new century. Cheap digital storage and computing speed, global mobile communications, a labor force in place in a globally connected world, and recent discoveries in artificial intelligence put you in position to turn the creation of social capital, something that had been limited to a few representatives of financial capital before, into an economic engine that marks the beginning of the decision economy. That economy will look different than the consumption economy, but the fundamentals for bringing about growth are the same as they've ever been. The fundamentals lie in Ford's three-step process in creating group persistence in the workplace.

Step One: Reconsider the Needs of People—to Share Purpose

Ford's interest in scientific management of the day differed from his contemporaries. While others focused solely on technology, time, tasks, employee input, and being nicer to employees to gain worker productivity and loyalty, Ford's first focus was to reconsider the needs of people to share purpose. He was the first to realize the relationship between social mobility and meaningful work, like the social meaning people lost when they left their farms in rural America. To replace what had been lost, he made a point of declaring a group purpose. He referred to this first part of the process saying, "Coming together is the beginning."

We have a similar need today to declare purpose to generate renewed social mobility. This time, though, shared consumerism is no longer producing a foundation for meaningful work. And not only will no Henry Ford appear to declare that purpose for us, our leaderless generations will have to declare it for themselves as a group. While authors and commentators (like me) will suggest relevance, transparency, and choices as the social-capital foundation for social mobility in the decision economy, you'll need to draw these conclusions for yourselves, as a matter of necessity. Leader-defined purpose won't work as a foundation for social-capital growth any longer.

In pursuing your job together, your interest in scientific management should differ from your contemporaries. While others will focus solely on technology, time, tasks, employee input, and saying yes to your colleagues to gain their cooperation, your first focus will be to reconsider the needs of people, helping them create and share their own purpose.

A good example for you to use as a model comes from the Mayo Clinic Model of Patient Care:

Patient Care

- Collegial, cooperative staff teamwork with true multi-specialty integration
- An unhurried examination with time to listen to the patient
- Physicians taking personal responsibility for directing patient care over time in a partnership with the local physician
- Highest quality patient care provided with compassion and trust
- Respect for the patient, family, and the patient's local physician
- Comprehensive evaluation with timely, efficient assessment and treatment
- Availability of the most advanced, innovative diagnostic and therapeutic technology and techniques

The first three principles of their Model of Patient Care describe the responsibilities of physicians and their other nonmedical colleagues *to one another*. Then, only after establishing integrated physician-led practice as their foundation, the model proceeds to describe those physicians' responsibilities *to their patients* and colleagues outside Mayo. Strikingly, the very last part of their model of patient care describes how they use the very best medical technologies and techniques. Most professional service firms' statements of client care today list those attributes in exactly the opposite order. It's up to you to **reconsider the needs of people to share purpose** by first coming to an agreement about what each of you *means to one another* before you move on to the second step.

Step Two: Redefine Value Creation—as Social Mobility

This second step in Henry Ford's formula for creating group persistence, and through it a rising middle class, was to redefine value creation as the creation of social mobility. This is what led to his employees being able to purchase the very cars they were building; they got to share in social mobility beyond what they had ever experienced. He called this persistence of human effort the "progress" of "keeping together" after the initial call to purpose—their "coming together."

Today, our leadership calls to inclusion are falling flat. Intuitively, our junior colleagues are disconnecting because they don't feel treated as equal participants in social mobility provided by the consumption economy. They are unable to experience the "progress" of "keeping together," because they feel like they are merely there to serve as a human buffer between the leader-defined purpose of our partners and the quality definitions of our clients, without being given real influence over the process of reconciling the two and creating equal inclusion and mobility for themselves.

A good example of this phenomenon is my accounting-firm partner–friend who retired early because he didn't want the pressure any longer of serving in that unequal social mobility world. His statement that "the firm wanted one thing and the clients wanted something else" is a stark reminder of the human toll of an unsuccessful social mobility strategy. He went on to explain that if it was just one pressure or the other, he could have managed working longer. But clearly, participation in this declining value-creation environment, even for partners, will continue to erode until you **redefine value creation as social mobility** for everyone in the decision economy.

Step Three: Redesign Your Growth Model—Through Meaningful Work

Ford called the third step in his organizational plan the "success" of "working together." He knew he could not redesign the growth model of his company without the inclusion of his workers, not just in the production of its products, but in experiencing the *meaning* of their consumption as well. Sustained human persistence of Ford's employees would be required despite the increasingly dehumanizing work environment of repetitive, socially isolating work. And to create that growth model, it was Ford's ability to bring meaning to work that helped workers turn an entire half-century of chaos and dehumanization into the foundation of the consumption economy of the twentieth century.

In today's economy, many business growth models look like Henry Ford's assembly lines, but without the positive social capital creation necessary to bring meaning to people's lives. They are auto manufacturers that produce piles of assembled auto parts instead of functioning whole cars that can take people to the beach. Or they are aspiring Mayo Clinics that vend random groups of medical procedures that can only accidentally produce outcomes for human beings. But what is causing this social-mobility dissonance, the race to achieve growth by seeing how quickly we can move consumer goods and business services around the world, or people following technology, is nearly over. Growth models must be redesigned so that people can follow people to create meaning in their lives.

A good example of workplace automation removing one job while creating another is in the simple but time-consuming process of estimating state income tax burdens for clients. New artificial intelligence products will easily accomplish what used to be repetitive and time-consuming calculations by people. It is exactly these types of activities, anything that can be made routine, that will be devoured by artificial intelligence.

But this elimination of a routine and mechanical task frees up talented people for more meaningful work. Human beings in the decision economy, and specifically those in this example, will not be managing knowledge and applying tax law to facts. Instead of that *knowledge management*, our New Giants will **redesign their growth model with meaningful work**—helping other people *assimilate knowledge*. That is where human and organizational outcomes occur, in the context of a wider decision-making universe that extends beyond the rote mechanics of crunching numbers, very much like the decision-making universe of our CFO that was overlooked when Anne discovered the $1.6 million tax deferral no one else in her office had seen.

Just like Henry Ford in the Followership Cycle before you, there is a century out in front of you—the decision economy—just waiting for you to define it. And the social mobility that will be created by its more meaningful work will benefit many generations to come equally, whether they moved to Detroit or not.

Chapter 8

Coming Together

The next phase of the Followership Cycle, people following people, will require the assembly of collective purpose from society. That all-inclusive reason to grow is what will make each member of the decision economy an equal stakeholder, generating the social capital that will build growth for people and organizations.

The underlying negotiation is already underway one transaction at a time in the trenches of our work and social lives. People are adapting to technology by gradually requiring each transaction to serve ever-higher levels of human need. But the process is slow and painful. Is there any way that we can speed things up to arrive at our preferred futures more quickly than the thirty years it took medicine to get as far as it has with its reason to grow?

I was chatting with Rick Kravitz, Managing Director of Content and Publishing at the New York State Society of CPAs, on the phone one day. We were discussing a practice management article I had written a year prior, titled, "The Great CPA Followership Crisis." I asked him if there was some way that we could meet with a diverse body of the Society's membership, to promote the idea of integrated practice; I wanted to help him create a foundation that could serve as a modern analogue to Ford's "Coming Together."

His response was direct: there was no such venue available. He went on to explain that a membership organization must be relevant to its members. And in the membership's eyes, that relevance sorted itself by the functional and industry specialization we see today on most of our colleagues' websites. He looked at the growth potential of his organization as being directly related to the number of things our profession knows how to do, all those services we see on the drop-down boxes on our websites.

They had a dizzying array of different interest groups in various disciplines, such as SEC reporting, financial services, real estate, nonprofit organizations, government, employee benefits, and many more. But not only did they have all these groups, they also had next-generation versions of some of them. The existence of these separate youth-oriented groups showed the stark social capital differences between the declining consumption economy and the ascending decision economy. Somehow, just like the rest of society, we have come to believe that segregating our professionals by age is a good people engagement strategy.

But, in his defense, these sorts of organizing habits are directly in line with the middle order of needs of people as laid out by Maslow. After our physical needs are taken care of, we are secure enough to begin affiliating with one another. This is where Rick's members live out their days today. With plenty of food and shelter to protect them, they begin taking care of their need for emotional security.

The first relationships we seek are those confirm how we define our unique selves. And who better to do that with than those who do exactly what we do? It is easiest to find relevance with others that have a common experience, both professionally and personally. And so specific groups form within organizations to address that need for the emotional security that comes from huddling with those who share our practices and beliefs. People outside of that group are irrelevant. As such, any potential for social mobility is severely limited because inter-practitioner relevance is the key to social capital growth outside of our specialties—just as Mayo Clinic has taught us.

But if the real social-mobility need is to come together to form a powerful reason to grow together, we must challenge ourselves to reach beyond physical and emotional security to reach for personal growth that can only come from preparing oneself to serve others. This is Maslow's highest order of the needs of people. And now that we've thought carefully about the true nature of social mobility and its relation to social capital in the decision economy we know that none of our specialist groups, like the ones that formed in Rick's organization, can create Followership growth alone. We need one another. For us to truly grow as self-actualizing people we need to collaborate and find meaning together so we can serve others, including those who never "moved to Detroit" as some of us began to follow technology during the last couple of decades.

As of today, the organization Rick serves has been able to adapt to the belonging needs of each of his specialist groups. But no place exists for them to collaborate with *other* groups, to think about the things Henry Ford thought about when he said, "Coming together is the beginning." They're all huddled with their own specialist allies, much like people in the rest of the economy. Unfortunately, growth through Followership isn't possible in an environment of isolation and irrelevance.

But how can we actually *do* that leading when people are separated in so many ways and the future place they're going to isn't yet known? It's not as though you can just call a meeting. It would be impossible to engage all of society that way. And even if we could, there would be no one to lead the meeting because purpose is no longer something that can be handed down by someone who's "in charge" who "knows what's going on." Fortunately for us, unlike what was available to Henry Ford, we have computer technology to assist us.

Cell phones were originally invented for people to follow technology. It is still great fun finding the latest apps that allow us to tap into new infrastructure in a completely mobile way, instead of having to sit down at a personal computer to execute basic tasks. They serve our basic needs in handling the transactions of our daily lives such as paying our bills and shopping at the grocery store.

But cell phone function has clearly moved well past serving only our physical needs for survival. The arrival of social media quickly turned cell phones into a way for people to follow one another to serve their needs for belonging and security. The arrival of Twitter and Facebook meant people could easily find support for their beliefs. We could find tribal communities for our unique selves, just like Rick's membership groups. Tribal huddling became the hallmark of modern social media.

But as of today, social media hasn't proven itself adept at helping people serve one another in a self-actualizing way. In fact, it would be hard to find anyone who believes it possible to create a successful social media site designed with the specific goal of negotiating purpose, quality, and accountability among people who *don't* share common beliefs, practices, and experience. There are all sorts of obstacles to the creation of such a site: trolls would destroy its serious purpose or there would be no incentive for people to willingly reach beyond the comfort of their own groups. Plenty of reasons exist for us *not* to believe that people would follow people in search of more meaningful lives than the ones they're currently living, lives that use cell phones to purchase creature comforts, such as coffee at Starbucks, or receive tribal support from their social media contacts, such as on Facebook.

Despite all the things we'd like social media to be, Facebook and Twitter have designed their business models for audience development, and not the durable shared purpose of a reason to grow for an entire society. Their platform designs are useless as a place for people to reconcile differing perspectives, becoming instead a hotbed for fake news and political tribalization warfare, a place for unidirectional spewing of "here's what I think, so there" instead of doing the hard work required to create a unified purpose. Both sites have proven weak at tamping down the margins of the most extreme effects of the tribal passions that fuel its revenue model. They do not appeal to our very highest angels—self-actualizing behavior that pursues a morally inclusive society.

But denying the potential of social media to do more than provide a place for us to like or dislike things would be to deny our very humanity. The arc of development of social media is already following the arc of development of the human beings that it serves. There is no reason to believe it would start by serving our lowest needs for transactional help in our daily lives, then progress to helping us with our tribal huddling for emotional security, and then stop there. It simply doesn't track with the progression of our human needs. There must be a higher purpose for it, even if its creators didn't plan for one. There *must* be a place for our New Giants to rise above creature comforts and their own need for tribal security, a place where they can all play an equal and leaderless role in defining the foundations of how we will create value and social mobility in the decision economy.

Medicine's slow evolution of crowdsourced purpose, quality, and accountability, leading to the state of practice today, happened with very few tools at its disposal. And yet, the way they built a reason to grow that included all stakeholders now serves as a case study in leaderless social mobility. In ugly transaction-by-transaction fashion, medicine found a way to replace a value creation system rooted in human permanence with a more sustainable form of permanence: shared societal purpose. They didn't have a social media platform to help them build that reason to grow. And so far, neither do we.

But we don't have to suffer the way they did. We can facilitate our own evolutionary process and get to that place much more quickly together than they were able to. And society will need us to move faster because there isn't much time left before artificial intelligence creates an overwhelming need for positive social-capital growth to help people follow people. As much as we'd like to think we've weathered the bulk of the storm of technology isolation, new forms of it are on the way that can only be combated by channeling that same powerful dynamic into a modern force that can spread benefits to every corner of the globe.

A Followership social media site is the only plausible way left for us to formulate, negotiate, and construct a functioning growth engine for social capital, based on the highest order of the needs of people. It must rise above the noise of other social media sites that are designed to prompt us to "unfollow" one another the moment someone says something that doesn't agree with our own sensibilities. As such, it is not really a social media site at all, but a twenty-first-century *social capital site* based on the creation and development of a durable shared purpose.

The easiest way to think about a Followership social capital site's potential architecture is to look again at how social mobility is pursued. In any Followership cycle, social mobility happens through the reconciliation of the unique self and its mobility compared to others, where meaning is determined. In an environment such as Facebook or Twitter, the first thing we do is define ourselves in a profile with personal information. Then we go on to describe our preferences by clicking on topics that are suggested to us based on tracking of previous activities.

Then we voluntarily associate with others, in hopes they like the same things we do. Sometimes they do and sometimes they don't, and so we then voluntarily follow or unfollow people to streamline that reconciliation of our unique selves with group meaning. At the end of that process, most of us have created a permanent, durable network of people that confirms our own worldviews, and describes social mobility to us in a way that conforms to our own beliefs. But this is not a social-capital environment equipped to sustain anything more than a subsistence-level consumption economy; durable networks of people won't be able to create growing global social capital any more successfully than company brands and employee engagement programs have proven capable of it. To build the decision economy, we'll need to share purpose with everyone.

As such, the architecture of a Followership social capital site must function quite differently than the way we create other social media sites. Instead of first defining unique selves who then pursue tribal support, it would start by crowdsourcing the definition of what is meaningful, a reason to grow, and only then seek to incorporate unique selves into that purpose. We've been trying to assemble positive social capital for years by doing it backwards. And it hasn't been working because of something called entropy.

Entropy is a physics term for system randomness, waste, and decay. It came to be more broadly used to describe the nature of systems in a broad array of topical areas, including sociology. The social capital premise of starting with a unique self and incorporating that self into a productive system involves, in effect, creating a whole new dedicated social system for every person in the world. And each of these systems require maintenance to continue functioning.

And like any system, each of those individual ones is subject to decay. That decay is measured by the level of energy needed for system maintenance that is then unavailable for productive work. The more energy that's taken up in maintaining that system, the less that is available for growth through meaningful work—the whole point of building the social capital system in the first place.

For example, in the consumption economy, system maintenance of our durable networks required an optimal amount of networking with clients, bankers, and other professionals, combined with enough internal meetings with staff and partners to create growth. The cost of this system maintenance used to be far outweighed by the overall growth in durable networks of people. Entropy costs were minimized.

But today, the disorder and decay of these networks mean their maintenance is overwhelming the growth they produce. Each meeting creates less value and traction than the one before it. Not only that, our response to a new generation of workers in search of meaning is causing us to say yes to them all the time. "Whatever you want, we'll give it to you. Just stay a little longer, okay?" When you add up the maintenance cost of this method of flailing at impermanence one employee at a time, the spectacular inefficiency of it becomes glaringly obvious. It's led to the rise of the talent-acquisition industry, which reflects a never-ending search for meaning by a population of young, unique individuals. And, in the absence of a reason to grow, their quest to find that meaning has grown increasingly disorganized and random.

When we think about social systems this way, it helps us to understand the benefits of the efficiency of constructing *only one* breathable system of social mobility, and then fitting unique individuals into it, instead of hoping Facebook and Twitter can help us move forward by assembling cultural tribes and then asking them to play nicely in the sandbox of the decision economy. When we reverse the construction of social mobility to reconciling unique self to group purpose, instead of reconciling group purpose to unique self, the cost of system maintenance goes way down. And the likelihood of success for people in their search for meaning and growth becomes much higher. That is what pursuit of a unified reason to grow can do for us.

As such, the primary design challenge of a Followership social capital site is to find a way for very busy people to share their human experiences in an efficient way. For it to be successful, social capital building needs to fit into our daily lives just as we've made room for Facebook and Twitter.

The first step our leaderless Henry Fords need to take to "come together" is to crowdsource their purpose, their shared reason to grow, through their own Followership social capital site. We know that today each company tries to do that through their mission, vision, values statements, brand promises, and employee engagement efforts. But the isolating effects of technology have eroded the social capital potential of those leadership and marketing mechanisms; they're no longer engaging stakeholders. So, rather than being a place to promote what amounts to brand as reason to grow, the first step for all Followership participants is to describe the real outcomes they observe in their daily lives.

To illustrate: for a specialized producer of billable time, perhaps someone on a leaderless team installing an enterprise resource planning (ERP) system, life at the office isn't quite as mechanical and meaningless as it might look to the partner in charge of the engagement. In fact, there might be rather a lot of observations that those young people have on the shop floor about how they, their colleagues from client offices, and system users felt about any given day's work. They're already thinking about them, and those thoughts are forming the meaning of their working lives, or the lack of it.

These stories about day-to-day experience reveal the cognitive and emotional dissonance between companies' statements of purpose and the reality of their lives. These points of human intersection produce thoughts and feelings that aren't currently being tapped as useful intelligence, because it looks too inefficient for us to bother with them as individual data points. And it would be too inefficient without artificial intelligence assistance. But if we think of the world as one big human brain, it becomes easier to visualize all our human interactions as the synapses of that brain. And collectively, those stories hold the code to a successful reason to grow. They are Ford's "Coming together is the beginning."

But establishment of a reason to grow is just that, only the beginning. Not only did we lose our purpose when we began crossing over from the consumption economy to the decision economy, but we also lost our hierarchical system of feedback—our ability to track the creation and maintenance of persistence through conversations in our tribal networks. Put simply, we don't get to talk to each other during the workday nearly as much.

As a result, we get stories such as my early-retirement friend who lost interest in working because he couldn't stand the pressure any longer of not having a voice when the firm and the client wanted different things. He felt as though he existed as a mere buffer between the financial-capital interests of his firm and the quality expectations of its clients. He became voiceless, and it took a toll.

These daily stories, all those frustrations, joys, and experiences we used to tell one another around the water cooler, need to be reassembled and organized and to have meaning extracted from them. In the coming world of artificial intelligence, doing so will require a nonhierarchical, machine-learning system of feedback. The objectives for this machine-learning are no different than those water cooler stories. They tell us a lot about the dynamics of why and how people persist in responding to one another; the measurement of this persistence is where quality is determined in a leaderless social capital system. The greater the persistence of effort, the greater the agreement on sharing quality. Ford talked about the importance of this persistence by saying, "Keeping together is progress." And so rather than coming from social media cheerleading for company values, this human persistence of keeping together can only come from equal access to that quality agreement.

And ultimately, any social-capital system needs to function such that the growth that it produces outweighs the costs required to maintain it. This will be key to finding a way to develop a programmed organizational response to the voiced experiences and feelings of people. This is the heart of evidence-based practice, based on a leaderless reason to grow.

For this, we will develop decision trees, the deep-learning neural networks of artificial intelligence that mimic what leaders used to do in the field, when they assessed and managed human persistence in real time in practice. The algorithms developed from "what people want" in the decision economy can be assembled and put into practice without requiring meetings that no one has time for anymore. The process of understanding each other will be much more accessible and genuine than when purpose was handed down from leaders and reinforced through buy-in meetings.

A social capital site is a place to provide equal access to everyone's differing perspectives. But, as human beings, we tend to view the world through the lens of our chosen tribal subgroups. It is this tendency that spurs most employees to assemble first by specialty rather than shared purpose. Tribal association is more comforting than the unsettling notion that social purpose might transcend our own beliefs and expertise, that true meaning comes from working together with people whose interests are far different than our own. For this reason, any Followership site must also correct for these tribal biases.

First, Followership outcome markers must be agnostic as to their source. One of the more glaring signs of disorganization in a profession's reason-to-grow is that people tend to view the size of their organization as a differentiator in describing their experiences. There is a strong bias about firm and client size, because it is an indicator of status. I am always told by management that smaller firm leadership problems are irrelevant to them. And yet human capital professionals describe them all as having the same problems, regardless of firm size.

This adds to the fracturing of common experience that already occurs through technical specialization. The needs of people don't vary by position, gender, dollar amounts, or entity size. No matter how big or small the organizations involved, people hold the workplace to universal social mobility standards, and there can be no room for bias in their extraction and assembly.

Secondly, any social capital site intended to serve an entire society must be morally inclusive. It stands to reason that critical mass in any social system has the best chance of success when participants are convinced that their own beliefs have been represented without moralization. Followership social capital sites are not a place for determining, legislating, educating, and enforcing moral behavior; they exist for a society to decide how they will proceed together to define and address common problems. They are *not* a place for the political reconciliation of unique experience and belief, but for *the creation and discovery of shared experience.*

For example, during the progressive movement of the early twentieth century, the consumption of alcohol was a hotly debated topic that was cast as a moral issue. The stress caused by people following technology to our cities had caused a public health crisis that appeared to be led by alcohol consumption. Prohibition was the result, lasting from 1920 to 1933. Ultimately though, alcohol was understood more completely by society to be a public health crisis caused by the social isolation and overcrowded cities, and not the moral failure of people there. Government analysis and legislation didn't lead to this conclusion, as evidenced by a failed attempt to prohibit its consumption. Instead, it was the shared experience of people over time that allowed everyone to eventually agree that alcohol abuse was a medical problem, not unlike how opioid addiction is finally being thought of today.

And lastly, Followership social capital sites must be sustainable. Not the kind of sustainability we might imagine, though. Sustainability as we think of it today is the pursuit of permanence, for example in ecological systems. Sustainability in the natural world describes the conservation of resources such that they never deplete through overconsumption, misuse, or other disruption. The goal of this form of sustainability is to establish a system that can survive in its current form indefinitely. We naturally think of sustainability as the defeat of impermanence.

This form of sustainability is also reflected in how we determine the risks to permanence in economic matters as well. We audit things, which is our way of "assuring" the public about permanence. But we also now provide services in something called "risk." This is the assessment of the likelihood that audit assurance we just provided might fall prey to impermanence. In the consumption economy, measuring this form of permanence of financial capital was a valuable decision-making tool. But this definition of sustainability won't meet our needs in the decision economy.

Today, sustainability is more usefully defined as the ability to adapt to impermanence. The technology disruption of artificial intelligence will render many of our industries unrecognizable, and very soon. The needs of people for meaningful work will be put under extreme pressure and will produce social disruption vastly greater than our current inability to engage employees and customers. Things are about to change dramatically. And our ability to lead sustainable lives, our ability to adapt to impermanence, will be entirely dependent on the social capital we create with a sustainably permanent, and shared, reason to grow.

All this coming change breeds uncertainty. And in the face of that murky future, it is a legitimate question as to whether we should start investing in formal Followership social capital sites yet. Mostly what we hear in the media are scary stories about robots, an unknown future, and unspecified calls to action to adapt now lest we all be left behind. We leave these articles with no sense of urgency, partly because we don't know what to do other than go back to work believing the future will reveal itself to us one day. We are busy today, and we will adapt when we must. This is a great way for organizations, professions, and people to fall behind the Followership efforts of the leaderless leaders that will get there first.

For example, Mark Cuban recently made the remark that the world's first trillionaire will come from implementation of applications in artificial intelligence. But in defining the reason to grow of the consumption economy, Henry Ford taught us that this won't be possible unless the needs of people are accounted for in the process. In that light, we can see that there won't be any one single inventor or implementer of artificial intelligence. It will be the leaderless New Giants, the Henry Fords of their time, who use it to define the reason to grow of the decision economy.

Chapter 9

Keeping Together

Our Followership social capital site needs to do more than just extract outcome definition data from its members to create a reason to grow. To achieve the progress of Ford's "Keeping Together," all participants must also *persist* in pursuing that reason, despite the challenges they may face. The key is keeping people engaged. And for that, our Followership social capital site must create access to quality for all participants equally. It must find the markers of human persistence that tell us where quality happens among people in an economy—not just with one another in the workplace, but among all parties to economic activity.

I once talked with a managing partner about the value of taking a Followership growth approach to creating engagement and inclusion in his firm. He agreed the premise made sense: he could see the self-inflicted breakdowns in their current leadership approach, which he described as trying to get people to talk to one another. But, he observed, the wrong people were talking to one another and following one another in unproductive ways. To make matters worse, the people who *did* need to talk to one another weren't doing so. Their accountability efforts were struggling to gain traction. There was no persistence of effort.

When he suggested incorporating my work into their management philosophy, the response he got from his management team was that they "already have too many meetings." It's a fair point. Many of us can remember attending "buy-in" meetings back in the Days of the Giants. During those meetings, partners, managers, and client representatives would describe a leader-defined purpose and then ask for feedback, to allow for something approximating equal access to the quality agreement. It was the consumption economy's version of inclusion.

The very best leaders could define purpose and give the appearance of equal access to quality without anyone in the room really knowing how they did it. The worst of those leaders held meetings that didn't inspire a sense of social mobility at all. People came away from them feeling as though they'd just wasted their time, because they didn't believe real input was invited or incorporated into a team plan. We all know how painful it is to sit in a room where a leader is holding court instead of leading.

There were two reasons for this. The first was that some participants in those quality discussions didn't believe in the purpose defined by the leader. It boiled down to people believing that "we're not doing the right thing." We addressed this part of the construction of our reason-to-grow last chapter; it is Ford's "Coming together is the beginning." If our New Giants have already defined what "doing the right thing" is, we no longer need to suffer meetings with leaders who define purpose that is inconsistent with the reason-to-grow.

But the second problem in those meetings arose when people came away feeling highly motivated by the shared purpose described by the leader, but not feeling as though their input was recognized or accounted for. They didn't believe they had equal access to the definition of quality, and secretly believed themselves to be mere pawns in a quality agreement made before the meeting ever started, like my early retirement friend. They didn't feel like they had a stake in defining quality. So, our Followership site needs a way to help people not only *come together*, but *keep together* in a transparent, inclusive, and automated way.

In the world of artificial intelligence, the progression of content from coming together to keeping together will be accomplished through aggregated user input. But today's social media feedback environments aren't designed for this; they're instead based on "liking" and "sharing" data and ideas, designed to intensify tribal beliefs and behaviors to form an audience. They are not designed to determine relevance in a morally inclusive manner. We all know the feelings of passion, revulsion, or annoyance we have whenever we see a "type yes and share if you agree" posting on Facebook. Stirring up tribal support for moral positions is useless to Followership.

To counteract those tribal tendencies, aggregated user input cannot be based on a tribal competition format. User input must be evaluated by other participants on a "most relevant supportive" and "most relevant critical" basis that looks more like Amazon's consumer review process than a Facebook posting. This process identifies content that is ready for promotion from Coming Together to Keeping Together status. Persistence in working together must come from evidence of sustained relevance to decision-makers, and not clickbait designed to generate "likes." This is consistent with our goal of an unbiased, factual, and morally inclusive future.

Demonstrating the ability to think critically about relevance in the differing stages of Followership also helps us identify leaders in a leaderless environment. Unlike leaders in the consumption economy who defined purpose and negotiated quality, the role of leaders in an environment of equals is to *defend* purpose and quality as they are defined and negotiated by all stakeholders. And to identify and promote these leaders, we need an automated way to stratify our participants based on their ability to think critically inside the three main areas of Followership development: purpose, quality, and accountability.

A good example of this is contained in assessment tools such as Predictive Index, DISC, and Myers–Briggs. These tools help people understand their own unique workplace talents to help them work more productively with their coworkers. Within our critical thinking feedback mechanism, machine selection will accomplish this for us automatically.

For example, we all know people who are exceptionally operationally focused. Some are design thinkers, have a high degree of emotional intelligence, or are passionate about their specialty's wider role in society. All these attributes are useful. But they are the *most* useful when applied at the right moment. Case in point, my daughter Anne has a very hard time listening to me talk about ideation and design because she sees the world as a list of jobs that need doing. The notion of using time during the day to imagine what the future might look like is a waste of her time. I, on the other hand, love to avoid working right next to Anne whenever I can. I like to think about design, people, and their motivations, and what a successful and happy workplace might look like tomorrow.

In the world of Followership leader promotion, Anne's feedback about quality design might come off as impatient and dismissive. She would tend to get lower relevance scores from other participants because she, like anyone, has a hard time thinking critically about things that don't interest her. But her operational relevance scores would be through-the-roof good. She is the queen of getting stuff done, and it would show in her assessments of operational matters in the Working Together section of our Followership platform. On the other hand, I would be happily tucked away at the design think tank, noodling on ideas in the Coming Together and Keeping Together Followership sections.

This automated promotion of leadership based on our unique productivity tendencies, rather than our specialties, is the living and integrated world of Followership. It is a place that combines the talents, skills, and perspectives of everyone involved, without any meetings whatsoever. It's like one giant human brain with the right synapses firing at the right times. Content flows naturally from tests of purpose, quality, and accountability, then advances through automated consensus to form concepts. The path is just as Henry Ford laid out: coming together, keeping together, and working together.

As a clearer picture of shared purpose begins to emerge from our efforts in the Coming Together section, we'll need to start gathering data on where all our Followership members currently spend their days compared to the ideals of the emerging reason-to-grow. These daily activities are expressions of their quality beliefs. We know that for everyone to persist in pursuing a reason to grow, the membership needs to be a broad cross section of not only decision-support professionals, but all stakeholders who rely on them, particularly consumers. It's essential to have a dynamic and living quality negotiation among all stakeholders trying to get better outcomes through better decision-making.

Today, Rick's members at the New York State Society can easily access producer quality in their specialties. It's their best thing because they are organized that way. Unfortunately, they have decreasing access to quality information from other practitioners and stakeholders. This specialization, along with the time pressure of their jobs, continues to put downward pressure on their ability to share quality experiences with one another and society.

So, aggregating quality beliefs in an automated way is crucial to forming a coherent system that can respond quickly to change. We will need this system to track the rapid evolution of quality as it promotes concepts from the Keeping Together section to the Working Together section of our site.

This real-time aggregation is especially crucial because increased social mobility through decision quality won't be happening in a static environment. Artificial intelligence will be replacing a lot of human decisions and actions over the course of the next couple of decades. And as people leave decision-making to robots and start making some new decisions themselves, perceptions of quality will change right along with that transition. This is because people value what other people do. If what people do changes, so will the things they see as valuable.

We can start thinking about quality sharing by building a Keeping Together matrix as it might have looked like at the height of the consumption economy. On the vertical axis, we can plot the volume of decision-making that occurs on any given day. And on the horizontal axis, we plot the origin of the data used in those decisions.

As discussed, the value of decision-making by people in the consumption economy was assessed by its contribution to permanence. For example, we measured the past by auditing old transactions and balances as a way of assessing the risk of change in the future. In the consumption economy, people handled knowledge management because it was too important to leave to computers. And as always, our beliefs about quality focused on our own human efforts, not on computers or anything else automated.

For example, I once spoke with a colleague at another firm about my firm's entry into the payroll services business back in the late 1990s. It's common today, but back then it was considered by some to be beneath us professionally. My colleague observed that he and his firm were focused on *creating value* for clients. Value in his mind was contained in analytics, the application of rules, laws, and regulations to facts that created recommendations geared toward permanence. The mechanical execution of transactions, such as payroll services, was menial work best left to computer software. His beliefs were not uncommon in those days, and yielded a Keeping Together matrix that looked like the one on the following page.

That bell curve tells us what we've known for a long time, that most decisions in commerce about what to do tomorrow are made using information we learned yesterday. But in the consumption economy, those

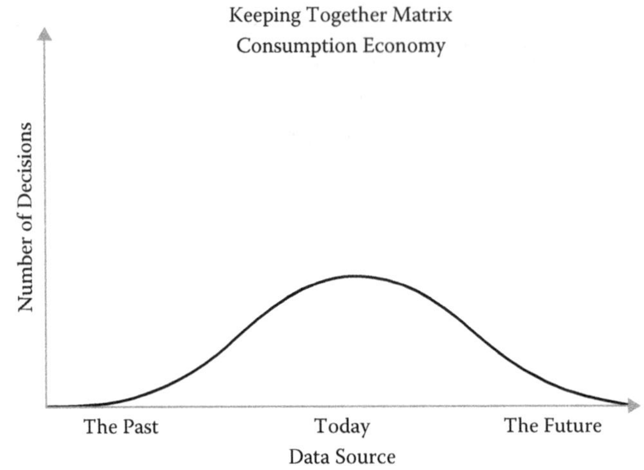

decisions were considered low value and unreliable because data was not considered to be information. University data processing courses routinely taught us that data didn't rise to the level of information until it had been extracted, parsed, and refined to the point of being meaningful. The quality belief was that, until human beings intervened, maximum value hadn't been created.

That alignment of duties and the resulting interpretation of value was not an accident. We always design our work to put human beings in position to add value after technology does as much legwork for us as it can. Technology's role has always been to relieve drudgery and elevate people so they can meaningfully assist one another in leading more meaningful lives. In pursuit of that, during the last forty years the relationship of people, computers, and information looked like the following.

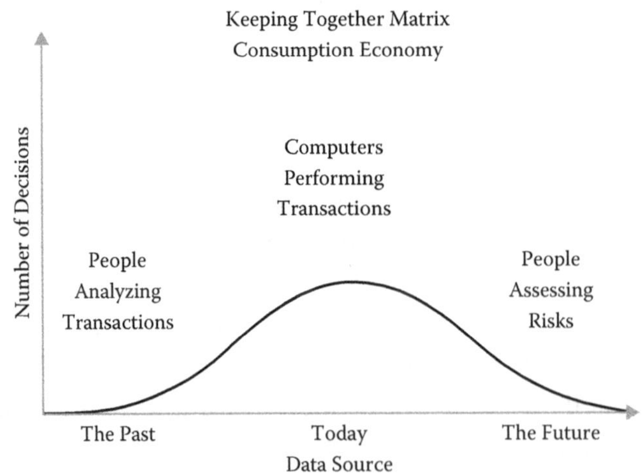

But this matrix began to show signs of wear as the Followership Cycle of the decision economy began to take hold. Information became outdated and irrelevant more quickly. And risk assessment that projected too far into the future began to look like mere speculation. As the pursuit of permanence began to give way to the adaptation to impermanence, increased time pressure began pushing the peak of the bell curve higher, squeezing the outlying areas smaller. Because of this time-pressured decision-making, payroll and other similarly automated transactional services began to increase in value, as people began to use that transactional data to make their operational and strategic decisions. So, our Keeping Together matrix started evolving to look something more like the following.

This is the resulting world of computer-assisted productivity we live in today. People working inside what we call accounting firms today work out in the margins of the bell curve, in analysis. And all other stakeholders, such as client representatives, lenders, and supply chain partners, work in the middle of the bell curve. From a traditional efficiency standpoint, it doesn't look all that bad. Everyone has plenty of technology to assist them in speeding up their important duties. And they all value their own personal efforts, because they understand their work and value their own unique selves. But here we start to see that onset of splintering and specialization: people no longer know much of anything about one another's work. So, they have very little need or ability to work with one another in an integrated way that builds social capital among people.

This is what we call technology "disruption." Not only does technology disruption disturb old business models, it disrupts the lives of people inside them, typically by reducing human contact. And these technology efficiencies create temporary problems for people. Not only does new technology disrupt the way we produce and consume things, it also disrupts the character and nature of the reasons we interact as human beings. As a result, people begin to lose their persistence together, which is the foundation of rising social capital. This is the cause of all our economic stagnation today. People are not following people. They are following technology.

Similarly, prior to the start of the consumption economy, Rockefeller, Carnegie, and J.P. Morgan disrupted the oil, steel, and finance businesses. All these disruptions were made possible by the relatively new form of capital responsible for wealth generation, financial capital. And they all led, just like today, to the isolation of people such that the social capital of the previous Followership cycle lost its ability to sustain economic growth.

Henry Ford understood how to respond to that disruption. Today and in the future, our version of his "Keeping Together" will be accomplished using the new tools of social capital sites and artificial intelligence. These efforts in purpose and quality engagement, our why and our how, can no longer be pursued in buy-in meetings.

But unlike Ford's efforts at engagement in the relatively stable environment of a manufacturing floor, our new leaderless generations need to "un-disrupt" the lives of people in an environment of perpetual and rapid global change. This rapid migration of people from old duties to new ones will change the very definition of quality. That's because the moment that any human duty becomes automated, its value drops immediately to a commodity price. It is the role of people that defines every Followership cycle's reason-to-grow, not the technology that supports them.

But the *catalyst* for the changing roles of people *is* contained in technology. Specifically, the rapid arc of change just arriving on our doorstep will be caused by artificial intelligence. Very soon, any duty that can be turned into a repeatable problem will quickly be turned over to it. As a result, people's jobs will change, and *where those people move* is where quality will be defined.

For example, knowledge-management duties currently performed by accountants will soon be assumed by computers. This means that our quality matrix will soon be completely devoid of people working in the production, dissemination, and analysis of information. This is what people today refer to as "The End of Accounting."

This redeployment of people won't happen overnight. Current estimates tell us that over the next twenty years, 40 percent of our duties could be assumed by artificial intelligence. And the Keeping Together section of our Followership platform will track, crowdsource really, that evolving definition

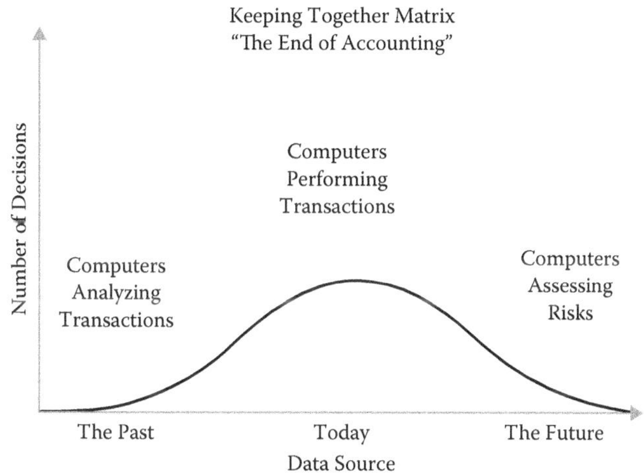

of quality in our work. Then, it will suggest real-time adaptations to those changes that will be promoted by consensus to the Working Together section for development and deployment. No meetings required.

Despite the prediction of the end of a profession, we know people spontaneously adapt whenever technology disrupts them. Once computers start handling the drudgery of knowledge management for us, the Followership future of people will be in *knowledge assimilation*, people helping other people take in complex information, assess risks, and then make decisions that pursue outcomes in a complex and uncertain world. This is how we'll adapt to impermanence. In that future world, the deployment of people should look more like this, with both producers and consumers of professional services functioning inside the bell curve of activity where most nonroutine human decisions occur.

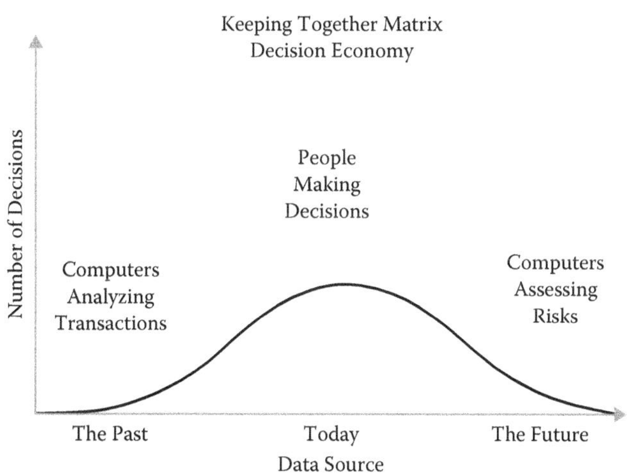

But the thought of losing work to technology scares us. And when it finally happens it hurts and can even make us angry. This is not because we loved our former duties, many of which were onerous or boring—pencil-drafting of tax returns, spreadsheet maintenance, or extending trial balances on fourteen-column ledger paper. Losing work hurts and scares us because we feel it as the loss of ourselves, the social mobility provided by our unique self and its relationship to other people. We were helping other people when we performed these duties, so they were valuable. *We* were valuable.

Real-time quality sharing, facilitated by our new platform, can push back against this fear by dealing with it in real time. The Keeping Together section of our social capital site will help us adapt to our workplace losses by perpetually reconnecting people to one another in newer, more meaningful ways. As robots replace us in the workplace, our only real option is to use those robots to adapt quickly by finding new duties to serve one another. This is how we will start successfully chasing quality.

In the last chapter, we learned about the need to track outcome markers. These are the feelings of people as expressed in stories told about their daily economic lives. Whether we are a decision worker, such as an accountant, or one of the many stakeholders who rely on them, such as client vendors, customers, investors, or workers, our daily lives are filled with stories of how we feel. The words inside these stories contain valuable data to be mined for the construction of our reason to grow.

Words such as "tired," "frustrated," "successful," "kind," "important," "together," "anxious," or "embarrassed" reflect our wish for meaning in the workplace. Each one is a momentary expression of whether we succeeded that day in finding it. And collectively, they express our wish for success as a social unit. At first glance, these words are a jumbled mass of emotion that would be hard for a human being to penetrate and make sense of. However, this is the sort of repetitive analysis that is child's play for a computer. As data accumulates, recurring word associations will give us feedback, and these trends and patterns can be used in constructing an idealized statement of purpose. It's the equivalent of building a living, breathing joint statement of mission, vision, and values for a growing social unit.

These outcome markers, developed in our Coming Together section, are then promoted via consensus to become a persistence marker in our Keeping Together section, where quality is negotiated. Persistence markers are repeated patterns of activity among stakeholders that demonstrate either human alignment, or a lack of it, in their daily pursuit of social mobility together.

Even if all stakeholders believe their reason to grow best serves their combined needs, a quality negotiation among those people is difficult because everyone's interests and beliefs are different. Each member tends to overstate the importance of his or her own contribution to the reason-to-grow. This is why Coming Together cannot proceed directly to Working Together; people first need a place to reconcile their unique selves to the greater group goals. If the Coming Together section of Followership is one giant, evolving statement of mission, vision, and values, we can think of Keeping Together as one big, permanent buy-in meeting.

A good example of this is Rick's organization at the New York State Society. All the activities of his organization are aimed at the value of the self, sorted by specialty, industry, and by age group. By addressing the tribal needs of people, Rick's organization is not at all unusual in that regard.

And yet we hear talk about pursuing a higher purpose everywhere in modern business conversation. Leadership in most companies is happy to tell its employees that a higher purpose is essential to leading meaningful work lives. But rather than build a living system to help employees find that higher purpose *together*, they basically tell their employees to each *go get their own*—believing that mere individual passion is the source of social mobility and meaningful work. That's because defining a combined reason to grow, and then negotiating what the pursuit of it means together, is a process that has been beyond the capabilities of the management tools most businesses rely on—until now.

All the more reason that the Keeping Together section of our platform needs to analyze repeated patterns of combined human persistence. And it needs to do this by plotting activities of stakeholders on something that looks like a three-dimensional version of our Keeping Together matrix. This analysis of human connection points will reveal some useful things for helping people and organizations grow together in meaningful and valuable ways.

First, it will tell us where stakeholders are not following one another, the misalignment caused by technology disruption, specialization, and time. A practical example of this phenomenon is contained in the $1.6 million tax savings Anne found for her client at tax preparation time. For Anne, it was a great victory. In the world of the client, it might have been a disappointing and disrupting event in her overall tax and financial plan for the year. Our Keeping Together site would reflect both sides of this transaction as a disconnection in time and specialty. Anne's data point would reside out in the margins of the bell curve, and the CFO's data point would live in the middle. There would be no blame assigned, or lesson plan developed, just the recording of another data point of disconnection for use in identifying patterns of quality growth or decline.

Second, recording this data will yield points of growing intersection among stakeholders as their expectations and duties to serve one another evolve to meet the needs of the reason-to-grow. These points of intersection can be used to promote content—accountability markers—from the Keeping Together section to the Working Together section, where practice tools will be developed for deployment in professional service firms and companies' decision-support systems. And because these process tools will have been vetted by the reason to grow and the quality-sharing agreement, the resulting tools will have a high probability of successful use.

Our Keeping Together section will also provide better career guidance to people than can possibly be obtained anywhere else in the world. Artificial intelligence will not only be able to learn existing persistence markers to project emerging job skill requirements, but it will increasingly be able to predict naturally occurring specialist career paths. Artificial intelligence will be able, in effect, to begin predicting the arc of the quality negotiation so that our leaderless generations' employment decisions can be made in a more coherent manner, rather than the currently random career paths in search of meaning. And lastly, but most importantly, our Keeping Together section helps our clients, their employees, and other stakeholders better understand their real choices in pursuing their own interests.

To see how a social mobility robot could assist a quality negotiation, we can observe similar efforts in another professional workplace today. In medicine, doctors gave feedback to patients, payers, and regulators about the challenges of meeting their expectations. Patients gave feedback to society about their quality beliefs. Payers compared costs of emerging medical technology and accepted practice to give feedback about price and value.

Over time, this process gradually revealed that the social determinants of medicine—the decision-making and actions of patients in their daily lives—was positively influencing overall public health far more than procedural medicine, our machine-read MRI scans, and our robotic surgeries. In view of that, medicine gradually adapted practices to deal with those human behavioral issues on a social level, to help reduce the number of people requiring intervention after they got sick.

We used to call this preventative medicine. More accurately today though, we think of it as social medicine. We use social information available *today* as the foundation for practice, rather than focusing efforts only on fixing the results of old behaviors. It is this redefinition of quality that has evolved medicine's reason-to-grow from curing the sick to the maintenance of public health. They accomplished this evolution without any help from a social mobility robot, though it took them a very long time. But in doing so, the arc of their Keeping Together matrix looks very much like what ours will begin to look like soon.

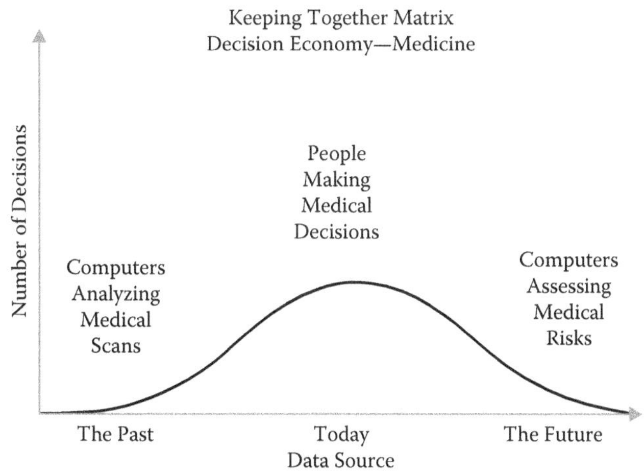

This gradual rise in universal access to quality sharing was the foundation for Followership in medicine. It allowed people to follow people in pursuit of the reason to grow, using input from everyone in society as a stakeholder. As everyone became included in the reason to grow and engaged in the quality negotiation, accountability became a motivator for change, instead of a dreaded enforcement mechanism perceived by most people as a tool used to promote the interests of ownership.

Followership sites you build can help accelerate the growth of social medicine. And that's because you will have learned how to build one for yourselves, to provide the global inclusion and engagement needed to serve the needs of the decision economy.

"Who's responsible to do this?" someone once asked me in an interview in New York, as I described social decision-making as the foundation for practice growth in the future. I was somewhat disarmed by the question because, up until that point, my belief had been that it was the responsibility of leadership. That's the way it used to work in the consumption economy. Although I fumbled the answer a bit, it came out as, "Everyone."

And by everyone, I meant exactly that. Colleagues in and outside of professional service firms, client employees, leadership, management, bankers, university professors and students, investors, regulators, anyone with the smallest stake in the reason-to-grow of the Followership Agreement of the twenty-first-century decision economy must be included, even the people who didn't "move to Detroit."

Chapter 10

Working Together

Ford's third step of "Working Together," or people following people, has always been the natural outcome of people pursuing common purpose through quality sharing. To help with that outcome though, our Followership social media platform must be able to produce new tools. But just as much as we need to conceive, build, test, and use the new tools that support the growth of social capital in the decision economy, we must also learn to set aside outdated methods from the consumption economy. This hasn't been easy to do.

For instance, financial statement auditing has lost its relevance for reasons that are no one's fault. First, time pressure has pushed almost every important business decision inside the bell curve of the Keeping Together matrix we saw last chapter. Most decisions are made using recent information. Financial statement auditing and risk assessment, however, live outside this high-relevance zone, since they analyze past transactions and assess risks to future performance.

But the effects of time pressure on our profession's future isn't the only reason our tools need to change. The more substantial reason is that almost all activities involved with assurance and risk will soon be performed by artificial intelligence. And as we know, once a task isn't performed by people, it loses its ability to build social capital. History shows us that the moment something becomes automated, its value falls to the commodity price of any other nonhuman input in business.

So, we know we need to replace assurance and risk services to remain relevant in the economy. We can do this by helping people become relevant *to one another*, so they can start building social capital. But we're so busy tending to the decision-making needs of slow-mobility financial capital that we don't have the time to tend to newer forms of capital that will be the key to growth in the decision economy. Even though organizations desperately need to produce this new social capital to keep growing, we're stuck trying to help them perpetuate themselves by tending to the declining form of capital responsible for wealth generation—financial capital. Today, newer forms of social capital assemble only randomly while we fail to address their construction systematically as the means to promote wealth generation and its expanding social mobility.

This is the reason a social capital platform must exist. In the Coming Together and Keeping Together sections, Followership will help us decide *why* and *what* we will accomplish together. And then, in our Working Together section, it will help us figure out *how* to build the tools of the future without needing to disrupt current operations during their construction. It is inclusion, engagement, and growth all wrapped into one high-efficiency, low-entropy system of social capital construction, deployment, and maintenance.

The tools we produce will allow our new leaderless generations to be accountable to one another in pursuit of the reason to grow. Just as outcome markers were promoted from the Coming Together section to become the persistence markers in our Keeping Together section, repeated patterns of human intersection in our Keeping Together section will produce the *accountability* markers that form the foundation for people to follow people in everyday practice.

Everyone in business has a different definition of accountability. People at the top of a management hierarchy hear it as a success indicator. People at the bottom don't think of success, but of being required to pay tribute to someone above them in that hierarchy. Without a reason to grow to support organizational growth, interpersonal accountability in most business has declined from being a positive common social mobility motivator to being the means we use to enforce a management food chain. When I hear a manager ask questions such as, "How can I get my people to be more accountable for results?" it tells me that social capital in his organization has died. Phrases such as "my people" used to be an indication of the breadth of a leader's social mobility reach in an organization. Today, that phrase conjures up cynical workplace imagery popularly depicted in television shows like *The Office*.

Happily, our new Followership tools will restore accountability to its rightful place in organizations, because it will no longer be focused on the mere growth of financial capital for the benefit of a few. It will be aimed instead at pursuing a reason-to-grow of an entire combined social unit, for the social mobility benefit of all. This Followership foundation will be much larger than the tribal partner practices of the past and will reinvigorate many terms that have lost their meaning in today's often-painful leadership environment.

Trust: In the Days of the Giants, trust was formed and enforced tribally by a leader. That leader relied on tribal members behaving in a manner consistent with promises he made about purpose and quality to other stakeholders. Trust was considered an expression of loyalty, and it was an act of disloyalty to share trust with someone outside of an organization without the permission of a leader. This is what held tribes together and provided for their growth, as well as growth in the economy at large.

Our New Giants know this form of trust limits growth today. Trust in the decision economy must be based on accountability, not to the whim of a tribal leader, but to pursuing the reason to grow. When people are freed from personal loyalties to pursue loyalty to a greater social purpose, the foundation for people and organizations to grow becomes infinitely more scalable. Trust, now focused on our one single reason to grow, is the Coming Together that Henry Ford talked about.

Team: We knew what a team was during the Days of the Giants; our durable networks of people. It took a long time to build each one, and it was worth the investment because they had great staying power. Social mobility, the ability to measure our unique selves compared to the group, was organic because it could spring easily from the constant interaction with the same set of people in a team over long periods of time.

But this social mobility formation is less useful with each passing year, because sustainable social and economic growth needs newer, more powerful, forms of persistence. There isn't time to build permanent teams for each new challenge to the reason to grow. As routine duties are reassigned to computers and people undertake more complex tasks, pursuing unique outcomes for other people will require teams that have unique skill sets and aptitudes. Each new challenge will require the efforts of new teams of specialists. The formation of these leaderless teams is our analogue to what Ford called Keeping Together.

Relationships: Previously, relationships provided social mobility through upward accountability to others within a tribal Followership Agreement. But newer, more isolating technologies and specialization began to interfere with our ability to establish these tribes. As a result, accountability to company goals became separated from being accountable to one another's social mobility. The consumption economy was no longer producing tribal relationships that could create meaningful work.

Now though, relationships will restore accountability to its rightful place as a means for people to help one another build their own social mobility. Relationships, now pursued through the new tools of accountability to a reason-to-grow, will be the ultimate successful expression of Henry Ford's goal of Working Together.

When Henry Ford set out to accomplish what is now credited with creating the rising middle class of the twentieth century, he didn't shrink from the isolating effects of assembly line technology. He not only embraced it, but also modified it to make it even *more* isolating and mechanical by introducing an assembly line that *moved.* But he recognized that each new step of automation put more pressure on workers. And that pressure needed to be accounted for in the lives of people working at Ford Motor Company.

Similarly today, despite calls by some for people to spend less time with their technology and interact with one another more often, the Henry Fords of tomorrow will embrace technology even further. The belief that more informal interaction among people humanizes the workplace is flawed. If it were true, then our office holiday parties, softball teams, and after-hours socializing would still be building more productive work relationships among people, like they did back in the Days of the Giants. But they're not.

Ford understood that human interaction that provided *social mobility* to workers was what mattered—not just spending time together, but persisting together providing for one another's social improvement. This led Ford to not only further embrace technology by producing more cars even faster, but also to make sure his workers were included in the social mobility that resulted. He accomplished this by famously doubling the wages of his workers, and getting involved in helping those workers achieve emotional security in their social lives outside of work. Those acts were credited with creating the consumption economy of the twentieth century.

Unfortunately, social mobility today can no longer be enhanced by our ability to buy cars or cell phones or anything else. Economic development must now serve ever-higher levels of human need to counteract the increasingly isolating effects of our new technology infrastructure. Followership has taught us that the foundations of human social mobility have been slowly inching up Maslow's hierarchy, from emotional security to personal growth. And because the rate of change in people's social-mobility behavior is caused by increasing technology isolation, artificial intelligence will soon make the motivational needs of people in our economy unrecognizably complex—even by today's already seemingly head-scratching standards.

But, far from taking away our social mobility, artificial intelligence will be our friend. Even greater automation than we experience today will free us up to help one another in more meaningful ways. So, like Ford, we will *further* embrace technology in the form of our social capital site, rather than shy away from it.

Accountability markers in our social capital site will tell us which efforts have effectively responded to the persistence markers promoted from our Keeping Together section. When people work together, whether it's in cyber-space or an artisan's studio, persistence is still based on trust, team, and relationships, but now in their most modern, leaderless forms pursuing one permanent and yet evolving, reason-to-grow.

Based on our discussion of persistence markers in the last chapter, we know that how we define quality as a society will soon start changing just as rapidly as people's jobs change—more rapidly than even today. We know that people ultimately value what other people do. And if we can't start predicting what people's work will be, then we won't be able to predict what quality will mean either. That's a problem for the stability and usefulness of our decision-making processes. If the quality definition is changing fast, the tools used to pursue it will need to change fast too.

So, our site needs to help us adapt when accountability breaks down and fails to produce the outcomes society expects. This adaptive capability is the new sustainability. And it functions far differently than old, static accountability methods where companies still try to get "results" from "their people." Instead, Followership's strategy is real-time adaptation to the evolution of purpose, quality, and accountability, which is soon to begin accelerating, assisted by artificial intelligence. The social mobility needs of people require that we start "chasing quality" rather than only grudgingly adapt to it after everyone else has.

When people try to be accountable, they succeed, fail, or fall somewhere in between. Our busy practitioners don't have time to analyze these breakdowns, make recommendations, or provide the associated analytics. All they can judge is whether they feel successful or not before moving on to their next client or patient duty. But if nothing is done to continually refresh purpose and quality, accountability among colleagues will continue to feel like slavery to others, rather than the motivating pursuit of everyone's social mobility.

When people use practice tools that fail the tests of the reason to grow, colleagues in the Working Together section of our Followership site need to reassess the decision pathways that led to the development of that tool. In some instances, the Working Together tools are simply either poorly designed or have implementation issues that need to be fixed. But sometimes, the tools no longer address the outcome or quality definitions that are changing rapidly. They may have become outdated and need replacement or redesign, as we see today with assurance and risk services.

This Working Together area is the crucial place where a dynamic system of purpose, quality, and accountability lives and breathes. Feedback from accountability performance will be crucial to the development and refinement of new practice tools. But it will also influence the sustainable evolution of the reason to grow and quality-sharing agreements. This in-progress social negotiation will determine whether assurance and risk services are redesigned, replaced, or some combination of both. Currently, this negotiation isn't happening fast enough to catch up to the social capital needs of the decision economy. The real issue today is not what accounting will look like in the future, but how quickly the decision-support function can get its reason to grow formed, so it can begin to help us find the answers to the questions we can't seem to articulate today.

Again, think of medicine: the field started a Followership approach well ahead of the rest of the economy. Fifty years ago, medicine was preoccupied with clinical intervention after people got sick; "fixing what's wrong" was the reason-to-grow. Patients and stakeholders lived and worked *outside* the bell curve of their Keeping Together matrix, in the low-volume area of medical practice decision-making. But everyone was happy because costs stayed in line. And the durable networks of people led by the Giants of medicine made us feel safer and more secure.

But costs began to increase with the demand for specialization and new technologies, and people balked at having to pay for access to whatever medicine could develop. Society had to start thinking about limits, and the quality negotiation among stakeholders intensified. Despite clear, objective evidence that medicine was improving its benefit to society, society *felt* like quality was declining. They wanted the social capital of their Giants back despite the better medicine of the day. The negotiation of the reason-to-grow began to account for the feelings of patients that formed their outcomes.

Out of this broadening negotiation, the tools of evidence management—specialists managing evidence of patient need—were used to control growth that didn't meet the standards of their reason to grow. This forced medicine to move away from relationship management driven by *patient wants* to specialist evidence management governed by *patient needs*. Medicine would not be allowed to grow further until it proved its commitment to the greater good of society, by committing to sharing a common purpose with it.

But a completely unexpected thing happened. Despite the use of a Followership process designed to *limit growth*, medicine began growing even more rapidly than ever. In fact, the share of U.S. GDP consumed by medicine nearly doubled from 9.2 percent in 1980 to 18 percent in 2010. In effect, evidence management in medicine was forcing more of its services to fall inside the bell curve of its Keeping Together matrix; not surprisingly, they've grown like mad ever since.

Right now, the accounting profession is stuck practicing outside the bell curve of its own Keeping Together matrix, struggling for growth that it hasn't justified to society. And just like medicine, we need an operational control framework that facilitates a social negotiation that can push our services more inside the bell curve of that Keeping Together matrix, where most decision-making occurs. That is where all the growth is; it's where people live unique and meaningful lives. But we cannot get to that wonderful place of growth and social mobility for everyone without a negotiation of our reason-to-grow first, just as medicine has done over the last several decades.

In medicine, changes to its persistence markers, how people persistently responded to one another's needs, began to influence *both* the reason to grow (Coming Together) and accountability tools (Working Together). It became the living and breathing growth imperative it is today because people followed people in a permanently evolving social contract—a Followership Agreement. But while their living system of social-capital growth was not assisted by artificial intelligence, ours must be; the global economy doesn't have fifty years to wait for us to prepare ourselves to serve the coming decision economy. That economy needs us to negotiate our own Followership Agreement much faster than medicine's. Fortunately, assisted by artificial intelligence, our leaderless, collective Henry Ford can start to quickly build a sustainably growing Followership Agreement to help create the rising social capital our economy needs to facilitate the growth of a new rising middle class.

To accomplish this, the first step in creating the Followership Agreement of the decision-support profession is to erase existing organizational and specialty lines; these have only hardened the outdated definitions of trust, team, and relationships in the consumption economy. Every institution that wants to be a part of this Followership Agreement needs to pursue a common, leaderless decision support reason to grow. Splitting leadership into separate, competing areas such as accounting, design, technology, data, finance, taxation, and government regulation has done nothing to contribute to the growth of meaningful lives for people, or by extension, the growth of the global economy.

Followership social capital sites can serve as the engine that builds that reason-to-grow. Their most important benefit is that people, all of them, have immediate and equal access to the source of social capital they need to build more meaningful lives together. Followership sites will allow them to make relevant contributions to colleagues and organizations around the globe through a single, common interface, regardless of specialty or markets. They are the means everyone can use to be invested in the same reason-to-grow, and they're applicable to a wide variety of organizations and institutions.

Professional Service Organizations

Today, employees in a typical professional service firm are classified by the client markets they serve. Then they are further identified by the size of entities they serve, and then their technical specialty. For example, it would not be unusual to have a mid-market, state, and local tax expert in the automobile industry. Unfortunately, that specialization leads that person to believe they are irrelevant to everyone but other mid-market, state, and local tax experts serving the automobile industry.

And these experts serve mostly nameless, faceless deciders-of-things in the automobile industry itself. Think again about that leaderless group of people installing the ERP system at a major corporation in Chapter 2. It was the group where no one was "in charge" or "knew what was going on." Each team member knew what their individual job was, but was unable to articulate how those jobs combined to positively influence society. This lack of common purpose is paralyzing to the social mobility of those young colleagues. Followership sites can help them knit that purpose together by crowdsourcing their experiences, and then encouraging them to access and witness the results that show how their efforts influence the shared reason to grow.

Universities and Their Students

Universities are also negatively affected by a lack of Followership social capital. Curriculum development has always struggled with the perception that it lags behind the needs of "the real world." Without access to this Followership social capital, this gap will grow bigger. Artificial intelligence is radically altering human economic decision-making, and it will be even harder for universities to keep up with each succeeding year.

To stay abreast of the economy, participating universities in your Followership site will have access to data on the evolution and current state of the reason to grow, for use in curriculum development that is responsive to this rapid change. This is valuable because of the disjointed and anecdotal way capstone and higher-level course work is currently developed. This curriculum is typically developed by professors using their own thought processes and experiences, based on feedback from the economy and colleagues about the integrative skills needed in the workplace and society.

While such processes produce valuable insight, they do not seamlessly and reliably participate in the wider, bias-filtered purpose negotiation happening more rapidly in the economy. As a result, students arrive in the workplace with the natural biases that human beings have when they work and learn in isolation from one another in society. Without Followership, education will lag behind the accelerating needs of people in the decision economy.

Financial Capital Markets

Financial-capital markets are struggling with the usefulness of decision-making material used by investors. During the early days of the consumption economy, when financial capital was the creator of social capital, intangible assets such as workforce in place and customer lists were relevant indicators of the value of a company. Investors could make reasonable inferences from the existence of these assets. The predictability of the actions and reactions of those durable networks of people were counted on as far more stable than they are today.

Now, in the decision economy, where social capital has become the foundation for the creation of financial capital, that predictability is gone. Evidence for that lack of predictability is laid out well in *The End of Accounting*.

In that book, the authors cite management's increased use of intangible assets, the rise of managerial estimates, and delays in the recognition of important events as being the primary reasons financial information has declined in relevance. The authors seem to recognize that, in effect, as pressure pushes more decision-making inside the bell curve of our Keeping Together matrix, we're being forced to *guess* more in our decision-making than ever before. A Followership social capital site can help investors and managers stay up to date on the rapid changes in social-capital formation.

Government Policy Makers

Government policy has always been routinely criticized as being unresponsive to the needs of its citizens. But the passing of law and resulting regulation is necessarily partisan, and we can't change that reality. This political legislative process produces a partisan see-sawing effect on policy that typically operates well behind the emerging needs of its citizens.

This slow march to the future will not serve our citizens adequately as the decision economy grows. The history of Followership tells us that governments typically don't deal quickly and effectively with the needs of each new form of capital as it begins to serve as the foundation of wealth creation. For example, the U.S. Securities and Exchange Commission (SEC) was organized out of legislation in the early 1930s only after the stock market crash that presaged the Great Depression. Its three-part mission today is described as to (1) protect investors, (2) maintain fair and orderly and efficient markets, and (3) facilitate capital formation. But to get to that necessarily regulated place, our nation had to wait for many decades of financial market abuse and resulting instability, which caused extraordinary pain and suffering for people.

Now that social capital is emerging as the primary foundation of wealth creation, governments won't be able to wait for decades of abuse and instability before acting on our behalf. All the elements of our government—executive, legislative, and regulatory—need to participate, not as an owner, but in the same way as any institution obligated to respond to people in the economy. There is no place in America today that exists solely to collect data to serve the social-capital decision-making needs of its citizens. Now more than ever, our citizens need this decision-making information to move forward *together* under one unifying and forward-moving Followership Agreement.

Social Capital Markets

We have a hard time thinking of social capital as having a "marketplace" of its own, but it does. It's a messy, innovative marketplace fraught with the same risks naturally associated with new forms of wealth-generating capital. Just like the early days of the rise of financial capital before it, no one knows exactly what its limits are or what its rules ought to be, if any. But just as when financial capital overtook land as the primary form of capital supporting wealth generation, the social capital of a reason-to-grow provides far more social mobility than its predecessor. It is accessible to anyone, and can be used for great good if we create and build it in an intentional way. And it can lead to great evil and suffering. Everything it can accomplish, good and bad, is coded into the needs of people to create meaning together.

But because social capital is no longer the organic and natural byproduct of doing business, it will need to be formed outside of commerce first as the basis for meaning and growth. If everyone's social mobility is not accounted for in the agreement, it will not perform efficiently in the marketplace. This not only includes institutions designed to represent us, but also each of us as individual human beings. As stakeholders of any form of capital capable of creating wealth, we all need better decision-making material than current forms of business, social media, or government are currently providing.

We are all stakeholders in a joint human venture. That's not some abstract, psychedelic, Age-of-Aquarius sort of statement; we are critically dependent on one another as people to create social mobility. It's how we are wired. And we need a way to account for that need in a regular, continuous, and meaningful way, despite our disconnected world of technology. Leaving that social formation to tribal huddling on Twitter and Facebook does not do justice to the great good people are destined to accomplish together.

Unlike the SEC's mission with respect to financial capital, there is very little anyone can do to protect investors in social capital. We cannot regulate its transfer, protect its owners, or mediate disputes among its stakeholders. People are free to associate with anyone they wish and to share any idea as the foundation for meaning in their lives. And the only way they can all move successfully from one Followership Agreement to another is by having better decision-making information. When it comes to social capital, the *one and only thing that society can influence* is assistance with capital formation—that is the goal of Followership, and that is the goal of our social capital platform—to create and nurture the reason-to-grow for the decision economy of the twenty-first century.

And the duty to create that future falls to you, our collective, leaderless Henry Ford.

Chapter 11

A Reason to Grow

Having looked at some of the details of our Followership social capital site, it's worth remembering the reason we need one at all: until everyone is included in the Followership agreement, people won't follow people—a crucial step on the road to a rising middle class and the social cohesion it will bring.

It's been nearly a half-century since the global economy produced positive social capital. It has been in decline since the consumption economy tapped itself out in the 1970s. Evidence of its death began to show up during the 1980s as internal company efficiency efforts and layoffs became increasingly popular as a way to sustain corporate profitability in the face of declining labor productivity.

At the same time, new computer and communications technologies emerged that would temporarily rescue global growth. Unfortunately for the middle class, this growth only benefitted those who built and deployed those new technologies. The Microsofts, Apples, Amazons, and Ubers of the world became symbols of great success, both financial and managerial—but they also came to be seen by some as responsible for the social unrest caused by the now-increasing wealth and income disparity.

The middle class does exist today. Its small membership is composed of the same people who populated it at this point in the previous Followership Cycle. Its members are a small band of professionals and technicians who assisted with the building of the economy's technology infrastructure and the people who "moved to Detroit" to enjoy rising incomes by following those new technologies. In doing so, members of this new middle-class foundation were able to consume more and better goods and services than the people who chose instead to remain in middle America to continue relying on a dying consumption economy for social mobility.

But these New Giants found themselves strangely unfulfilled despite their own success. Just as their historical counterparts who moved from farms to factories over a century earlier, they too suffered from the isolating effects of a newer workplace. As their daily transactions became increasingly impersonal, isolation grew and social mobility slowed. They had become a small middle class made up of unique, talented, and successful specialists who no longer felt they were producing meaningful work together.

It is no one's fault that the consumption economy died as the foundation for a rising middle class. The Followership Agreements that support this process, the social contracts, have life cycles just like everything else. Cheap oil, steel, electricity, and railroads spawned a technology and people environment where labor could finally be included in the middle class. But that socio-industrial infrastructure could only serve as the foundation for social capital until a better one came along.

One could argue that Rockefeller, Carnegie, and J.P. Morgan lived too long ago to be relevant to our New Giants. They are both lionized in the dated yet mythically powerful, male-dominated narrative of "The Men Who Built America," while also despised as the Robber Barons of a distasteful past who showed little regard for the health, welfare, and social mobility needs of the people they employed. It sounds outdated, but history has a way of repeating itself. Figures like these appeared again. Only the names were different.

Gates, Jobs, and Bezos filled those same roles in our latest socio-industrial regeneration. They all acquired their wealth when technology followed technology, and when people began to follow that technology. Just like Rockefeller and Carnegie before them, they too have been alternately revered as titans of industry—creators of what is new and disruptive—and despised by others as parasites feeding on the declining social capital of the previous Followership Cycle—not bothering to contribute to the construction of newer forms.

As it turns out, neither of those narratives is true or helpful in showing our New Giants their collective role, their place in history. Neither celebrating or despising the Giants tells the New Giants what they ought to do about declining social capital. As such, all these historical figures both recent and ancient, are irrelevant. They should be placed in the history books as examples that can instruct people at the beginning of a future Followership Cycle—when technology again follows technology to create the next major socio-industrial regeneration.

This is because all those titans of industry *really* did was create a new technology infrastructure that would serve wealth creation and social mobility for a new rising middle class. In Rockefeller and Carnegie's case, they contributed to the foundation that paved the way for Henry Ford to appear to almost single-handedly create the consumption economy of the twentieth century, by allowing people to follow other people. And now, in our current Followership Cycle, Gates, Jobs, and Bezos have contributed to creating the technology infrastructure that our New Giants will use to become the collective Henry Ford of their time.

It is this historical and sociological backdrop that tells our New Giants about their destiny and, in the process, defines the reason to grow for a new century. We are once again on the cusp of Followership transition, on the verge of changing the very foundations of human social mobility. In this new decision economy, it will be up to our New Giants to build the new living, breathable growth imperative of their new century.

To do this, the first step is for them to define themselves as a profession. The decision-support function is currently spread out and separated across many disciplines. Pieces of it exist in every department of our commercial, nonprofit, governmental, educational, and professional-service institutions. Decision support does not yet exist as one profession with a common reason to grow. But the New Giants are learning this disorganization is a key reason their work lives lack meaning. They know their social mobility hinges on helping people follow people to create their own—and to successfully do that they need to be relevant to one another first.

Because of this reality, the first call to action *must* be to get organized. As our example of Mayo Clinic's Model of Patient Care clearly demonstrates, *our New Giants will not become relevant to society until they first become relevant to one another.* This serious work requires an artificial intelligence (AI)–assisted social capital platform because our busy professional lives no longer allow for buy-in meetings or water cooler discussions. And our New Giants know everyone must be included in the social-capital negotiation for it to provide social mobility to all. But just like with any grassroots movement, this people infrastructure is something they will need to *fight* for.

The need for grassroots activism is well illustrated in the Followership Cycle that marked the beginning of the consumption economy. The building and deployment of new industrial infrastructure lasted roughly from the end of the Civil War to around the turn of the twentieth century. This was "The Gilded Age," when social inequities of the day were thinly disguised by the wonders of new technology. Widespread problems and a lack of social mobility stemmed from the isolation caused by the same technologies popular culture was celebrating.

But eventually people began following people in response to these social problems. This marked the beginning of what came to be known as the Progressive Era in the United States. From around 1890 to as far as the New Deal in the 1940s, grassroots movements materialized in a variety of institutions, with goals of reform aimed at coping with the stresses of urbanization and industrialization. Although the federal government got involved later in the movement, initial efforts were very much local: professionals, educators, institutions, and local governments got actively involved in addressing the social problems created by the new manufacturing technologies.

Our New Giants face a similarly "gilded" moment today. Just as the regeneration before it, technology of today is frequently touted as the solution to people's social-mobility needs. These technologies are big, amazing, and uniquely wonderful—meanwhile, people are quietly left to feel small, irrelevant, and replaceable. The loud cheerleading that pretends this isn't true, the thin veneer that makes up the fiction of our own Second Gilded Age, was rather unceremoniously exposed during the U.S. national elections in 2016. This fiction will continue to be eroded as the New Giants enter their own Progressive Era, to address the problems that will be caused by the newest elements of industrial regeneration—most notably, AI.

The previous Progressive Era took decades to spread in the early twentieth century before elevating to the level of national consciousness and action. With the Internet, the grassroots efforts of the New Giants don't have to remain local for nearly as long. Social capital sites will give them the opportunity to benefit mankind and witness the results of their progress all within their own lifetimes.

But our New Giants will need to do their homework to make a good argument for why proactively building social capital is crucial to the growth of both people and business in the decision economy. They need to be able to demonstrate how helping people be accountable to one another is an important *first* step to helping them be accountable to their jobs. And this plan must be cost-effective.

Organizations today allocate resources to the Followership problem by funding extensive marketing campaigns to customers and engagement campaigns for employees. This strategy, which proposes their brands as a reason to grow, isn't working because most people see these efforts as marketing fluff—a thin gilding on what they think of as their real lives. Your proposal to organizations must be based on a new strategy, one that connects marketing campaigns and employee engagement as two individual parts of a single problem: a lack of Followership caused by a technology-induced decline in human connectedness. Any solution must be designed to functionally reconnect people, not just talk about what a good idea it might be in their spare time.

Seen this way, an argument for a social capital site is simple economic efficiency. Resources currently spent connecting people to one another are ineffective and inefficient. All that needs to be done is to move resources from inefficient uses in marketing and human capital to more efficient uses in social capital construction. Loyalty and engagement produced by this Followership approach will far outstrip the benefits of internal and external marketing programs that have been failing for decades.

Of course, as you make the argument for your profession's role in building the world's "people infrastructure," there will be challengers. In addition to disbelief by some that building social capital *before* starting to buy and sell stuff to one another is a valid growth strategy, there will be other professions and institutions that will try to lay claim to the social capital construction project of the decision economy. Governments, educators, news media outlets, and ideologies of all kinds will declare themselves to be social definers and builders of the new century. While they will all have a role, we know that the decision-support profession alone will make the truly defining contribution to the rise of the decision economy.

The thin, shiny veneer that shielded our technologies from a more critical examination has recently been stripped away, revealing a broad disconnect in public opinion as to what exactly should be done about the evolution of the economy. Much like in the election of 1896, the election cycle of 2016 galvanized highly polarized social-capital beliefs in a debate of largely irrelevant issues in a public arena almost completely devoid of factual argument. This polarization was not accidental. In both elections, political opponents shamelessly manipulated vulnerable believers on both sides of the social capital argument to get elected; they did this not to help build a morally complex and inclusive society, but so that one side could win the right to make policy.

This highlights something crucial: government has never been the creator of social capital. That is the role of ordinary people finding ever-newer ways to create wealth and social mobility by pursuing purposeful lives together. This fundamental truth does not make government evil or unresponsive. It merely makes them irrelevant to the initiation of the negotiation of purpose, quality, and accountability in the transactions of our daily lives. Government will regulate those transactions as referee, but it will never create them. That's your job. Henry Ford taught us that people first *come together*, then *keep together*, and then *work together* in a spontaneous, adaptive response to filling their human needs; your social capital site will facilitate the ability of people to follow one another. The only things people will need to create social mobility in the decision economy is the presence of other people and equal access to objective decision-making information.

Governments do not provide this accessible decision-making information to the populations they govern despite their being in the best position to do so. This has led to private citizens having to pick up the slack. For example, former Microsoft CEO Steve Ballmer recently created a website for just such a purpose. It was one the government could have easily created itself, using information it has already produced. His nonpartisan organization, called USAFacts, claims its mission as, "a new data-driven portrait of the American population, our government's finances, and government's impact on society" that "rel(ies) exclusively on publicly available government data sources." The organization further asserts its mission as the very same as the mission of our New Giants: "We don't make judgments or prescribe specific policies. Whether government money is spent wisely or not, whether our quality of life is improving or getting worse—*that's for you to decide*" (emphasis added).

By some accounts, Ballmer invested $10 million in the project so Americans could see what happens to public money in an accessible way. Such a project would have hardly been too expensive for the U.S. government. And yet it hasn't provided this in the same way it provides nonpartisan information to Congress through the Congressional Budget Office. Governments, it seems, are far too busy getting elected and trying to make policy to get in the business of having an informed populace. As such, that job will fall to our New Giants.

Similarly, the news media won't lead the creation of decision-support infrastructure. Belief in the objectivity of traditional news organizations has steadily declined, and it has eroded our confidence in it over the last half century. One could argue this was caused by the Internet, but the history is much deeper than that. It reveals that the job of news organizations has never really been to inform the populace with fair, balanced, and dispassionate analysis, but to challenge power.

Walter Cronkite was held up in the 1960s and 1970s as an example of a fatherly, wise, and balanced news anchor, and was called "the most trusted man in America." This concept of "the news" seems quaint by today's standards. But Cronkite occupied this space because this era happened to be the peak of prosperity in the consumption economy. During that time, labor was broadly included in that prosperity; people of limited education could graduate high school, find a job in one of the many factories operating then in the United States, and obtain social mobility in a way that hadn't been seen in society before. This prosperity lulled society into a false sense of security about truth, morality, and trust. We didn't have that much to fight about economically among ourselves, so we trusted one another. And we trusted Cronkite.

But as the saying goes, when the watering hole begins to dry up, the animals around it start to look differently at one another. When one Followership Cycle ends and another begins, we see great unrest. It is during these times the news media's true calling is revealed: to give voice to the frustrations of readers and listeners by challenging power.

The term yellow journalism was coined in the 1890s to name what was becoming the "fake news" of that restless time of Followership transition. It served the same purpose as fake news does today: to inflame a frustrated population of people who believe themselves to be aggrieved parties in the catastrophic and involuntary loss of their social mobility. During times of major Followership transition, the press is a wild, messy, and power-partisan place that doesn't focus on the boring job of providing decision-making information. As both vendors of popular frustration and relentless challengers to political power, they cannot do the job that the decision-support profession must.

Education is also poorly positioned to lead the decision economy. There was a growing belief during the Progressive Era in the early twentieth century that public education could propel society forward together. An increasingly educated and rising middle class was advocating for reform, so the natural belief was that public education itself would create rising economic progress. This belief missed a crucial point: people cannot be *enlightened* out of the way that they *feel*. People must experience the benefits of inclusion in economic progress *first*, before they will demand better education for themselves and their children. The progress in Followership, made by the Henry Fords of the world, created the demand for more education. Not the other way around.

Our current efforts to create a cohesive society, especially one as diverse as the global economy is producing, cannot move forward together until each citizen first *wants* that education. The growth of "alternative facts" continues to frustrate a population of scientists, educators, and analysts who can't seem to figure out why some people don't want new information. Some of these experts publicly declare resistance to science and education is intellectual laziness, rather than recognizing it as a symptom of the frustrations about a lack of inclusion in newer systems of social mobility.

Rising inclusion in the consumption economy created a call for better education, and so, too, will rising inclusion in the decision economy. But this result can only occur once that economy has been constructed, and social capital is more broadly available. This requires a better decision-making apparatus to aid the process of Followership.

Then, who or what is left to take the lead in social-capital growth with truly moral, factual, and objective decision-making material? Beyond government, the news media, public education, or any other institution we thought informed our lives and protected us, there will be no new teller-of-truth to guide us forward as a unified society. There is no new ideology, no new "ism," that can rescue the global economy from needing to create a cohesive society from an unprecedentedly diverse population, using newly constructed social capital. All that any ideology can possibly do, whether it is founded in faith, governance, social systems, or economic belief, is create tribal units by boiling down the moral complexity around them into simple, enforceable moral codes and then invite members of other ideologies to abandon their own to join them.

We know that tribalism, durable networks of people, can no longer create adequate growth for people, organizations, or nations. Having worked our way through all the institutions and ideologies we thought were responsible for us, all we have left is our collective selves to dig our way out of this together. For a new and rising decision-support profession, a cohesive reason to grow lies in leading this dig.

So far, we have resorted instead to using our institutions and ideologies to declare war on one another's beliefs. This has shredded the social fabric such that its members now believe forward progress will come by winning elections. When times are good, these institutions can *appear* to be a part of the system that ordinary people use to make decisions. But during the hard times, they're going to fight one another, because that's what we ask them to do.

The future of our New Giants of the decision-support profession is not to identify an unknowable future by assessing risk, turning it into an ideology of permanent sustainability and then proceeding to enlighten nonbelievers with assurance services by auditing it. Society doesn't need this guidance to achieve social mobility—it needs decision-making information. Not only do truth and permanence not exist today, they didn't exist in Walter Cronkite's day either. It only *felt* that way. The foundation of social capital—the reason we persist in our efforts together as human beings—is an emotional response to our daily lives, not a rational one.

Steve Ballmer's USAFacts is an example of a first step in a process that will lead the construction and growth of social capital in the decision economy. A website where people can easily retrieve nonbiased decision-making information is a wonderful idea, but it falls one step short of putting an entire society in position to decide its future together. The site is static, and can only vend information to individual people who voluntarily go there to retrieve it, people who know what the right questions are that need answering.

In a modern Followership world in which everyone in the global economy must follow everyone else to the future, AI will allow for something that the technology limits of the past would have made impossible: *technology can now follow people.* It can record their thoughts, experiences, and feelings in a perpetually evolving way, capable of assembling the combined will of entire professions, institutions, industries, and nations. As such, just like the interested parties today going to Steve Ballmer's USAFacts site, it will help the decision-support profession, and by association everyone in the world, *start to agree on what the right questions are* that fulfill the social contract of our reason to grow.

Any news story we see today about AI has two parts. First, the story discusses the amazing ways AI can assume people's current duties. Secondly, the story then talks about the "darker side" of AI, with a lot of handwringing about malevolent forces akin to George Orwell's Big Brother character in his novel *1984*. We never get the third part, the real story of how AI will assist us in negotiating social capital and assembling the tools of social mobility quickly enough to respond to the coming chaos about to be created by new and unprecedented technology-induced human isolation.

The first profession that needs to make this move toward active social-capital generation is, unsurprisingly, the one we used to think of as the accounting profession—the one that must now become the decision-support profession. Today, accounting is wrapping up its Followership role of the twentieth century where, alone, it provided decision-making information to investors and managers who then used that information to promote the interests of financial capital—thus building the durable networks of people that grew as a result.

Increasingly going forward, the newer and more effective decision-support profession will be providing decision-making information to far more people than investors and managers of financial capital; it will be every single Followership participant in the world. Everyone will have a stake and a voice in the construction of the social capital of the decision economy.

And far from becoming irrelevant, as predicted by *The End of Accounting*, the decision-support profession will be the *architect* of the decision economy. Instead of people continuing to follow technology, technology will now serve *you* as you serve the decision-making and social-mobility needs of every member of society. You will be our New Giants Rising.

Index

W

Y

www.ingramcontent.com/pod-product-compliance
Lightning Source LLC
LaVergne TN
LVHW080656011026
849160LV00014B/1448
* 9 7 8 1 1 3 8 6 2 6 4 9 2 *